# THE MINDFUL MENOPAUSE

## THE SECRET TO BALANCE, VITALITY & CLARITY THROUGH THE CHANGE

CLARISSA HUGHES

ISBN: 978-91-639-9416-6

## DEDICATION

To all the women I've met, shared laughter and tears with along my menopause journey. Thank you for being you.

# Contents

# HOW TO USE THIS BOOK

You can use this book as 'support' that you can dip into throughout your menopause or if there are particular aspects that you feel that you want to focus on. It can also be used as a course that you can do over an eight-week period one chapter at a time. In the Appendix, I have set out how you could do this in a step-wise manner using selected practices.

The book is broken down into nine key chapters, and each chapter contains several of these elements:

- **An inspiring poem** to set the mood and lift your spirit. These are poems I use with my clients in private and group session.
- **Background information** on the theme of the chapter and it's relevance to the menopause
- **Stories** that are based on interviews with women and a few men who have shared their experiences of their menopause or those of their partner
- **Meditations** focusing on the theme of the chapter. I aimed to make these as accessible and straightforward as possible so that even someone who is not a regular meditator can fit them into their busy lives
- **Short Mindfulness Exercises** that are intended to help you along the journey. They include journaling, visualizations and short habit changing practices. I tried to make them enjoyable and effective.

The first seven chapters focus on a step by step approach to bring different aspects of mindfulness to your menopause experience. Chapters 8 and 9 are focused on how to live mindfully not just during the whole menopause stage but beyond. I hope that supports you in making mindfulness a part of your daily life, where I believe it has the greatest capacity to bring every one of us into feeling calm, connected, confident and content.

Now let's get ready to dive into the Mindful Menopause.

# INTRODUCTION: WHY THE MINDFUL MENOPAUSE?

For as long as I've known I've been curious about people's behavior, their thoughts and wanting to help others. Originally I wanted to be a child psychologist but met opposition from my family and so drifted into a science career which I engineered to connect me to work involved with the human mind. My career blossomed, and then in my mid-thirties, I got married and shortly afterward my beautiful son was born. But the problems in our marriage quickly surfaced. My now ex-husband had a significant problem with alcohol which anyone who has been married to an alcoholic knows places strain on family members. On the surface, I had to appear to have it all - senior roles in world-class corporations and all the material things that came with that. Underneath was a different story. Life felt demanding, I spent a lot of time trying to please a lot of people and yet often ended up simply feeling anxious, guilty, inadequate, tired and overwhelmed with it all.

In my early 40's my mother developed senile dementia and having been brought up to conform I took on the role of carer. I felt like I had to say Yes, despite my inner voice screaming NO I can't cope with any more responsibility. But since I didn't understand the concept of self-care, and I didn't know how to ask for help, I knuckled down and added this extra role to my already chaotic life. I'm not sure if it was pride, fear of being seen as less than perfect or something else.

When I turned 45 things began to unravel after the death of my mother. There was a traumatic end to my marriage and a move to Australia with my seven-year-old son. It happened so fast so spontaneously. I felt I woke up one day and said, 'I can't do this life in this way anymore.'

But of course, running away is never the solution. Instead, I replaced one set of issues with another. Life seemed like an endless round of work, eat and sleep. At the same time, I became peri-menopausal, though at the time I was completely unaware that this stage of life even existed. My experience of the menopause had been that of my mother's which had placed a strain on our already fragile small family. She developed migraines, became very anxious and increasingly withdrew from being social. I became an adult at 13, as I had to take control of many aspects of the day to day in our home.

My menopause started with my weight ballooning, and I indeed had periods that were heavy, uncomfortable and unpredictable. This made me felt inadequate and insecure. These feelings weren't helped by working in corporate cultures where everyone on the surface behaved as if they had their 'shit' together. I ended up comparing my insides with other people's outsides.

I tried to conform, to look a certain way that would gain approval. I hated the way the menopause was changing the way I looked, so I dyed my hair blonde, got fake tans, did obsessive gym workout, Botox and the rest. Well, you get the picture. I started to live a certain lifestyle which led me into $50,000 credit card debt I couldn't or didn't want to find a way out of. I had a wardrobe full of designer clothes, which I regularly sold at the end of the month to meet my grocery bill. I bought a bigger car which I rarely drove but added an extra $1K for my monthly bills.

Night sweats and feelings of breathlessness created sleepless nights. And once awake my mind would churn over all my problems, keeping me up for hours until I would fall asleep at 4 am only to wake up at 7 am to do it all again. I was exhausted, and my health began to suffer. My blood pressure increased, and I had to go onto medication which was increased 3 x in a year. Stress and the menopause are not great bedfellows.

The 'real kicker' came when I changed jobs. I was offered a fantastic position in a company where I genuinely liked the people and felt a rapport. But the salary was lower and because of 'my supposed lifestyle' needs' I declined it. I 'wanted' more and accepted a better paying role. However, four weeks in, I realized that I was in the wrong environment. I had made a mistake, but there was nowhere to go. Senior positions in my field are few and far between in Australia. I felt trapped, tired and losing my passion for life. I suffered a burnout - not the classic adrenal fatigue but a slow draining of any remaining happiness from my life. Negativity took hold, and I didn't see the joy in even the small things.

On top of that brain fog kicked in and I developed a habit of not hearing people, going blank and giving the impression that I wasn't listening at work or to my son. It still pains me to remember how many times Tom said to me "You never listen, Mum". I had no mechanism to share what I was experiencing. And when a colleague attacked me saying quite bluntly, as only an Aussie can, that I made people feel uncomfortable and they couldn't trust me. I was devastated, angry, defensive and withdrew more and more into myself.

So how did I turn around? At some point in our lives, we have to stop running from ourselves. For me, it was small steps, and chance encounters that led me to become fully aware of my inner critic and the damage of not being true to myself had done. The suffering it had inflicted. I was in my early 50's and still experiencing many of my menopause symptoms even though my periods had dropped to an occasional trickle, the brain fog and night sweats were in full force. I had always loved yoga and meditation, but life got in the way. My son came first always, and because I had so few friends, 'me-time' didn't happen, as I had no one to help me out with him. When he reached high school, I felt compelled to carve out some 'me time.' I joined a small free meditation group that met for an hour once a week in a beautiful beachside park. I felt connection and support for the first time in 15 years. And a chance encounter with a wonderful woman, Heather, led me to mindfulness. 4 months into the 'new' job, I enrolled on an 8- week mindfulness program, mindfulness-based stress reduction (MBSR).

I became aware that to start to thrive in my life I needed to slow down. I needed to take responsibility for my choices and actions, rather than feeling like a victim to my life. I needed to learn how to say no to those things and people that didn't align to what brings joy, meaning, and purpose to my life. I needed to find some self-compassion and practice self-care!

I went on a weekend retreat on a Mindful Movement with Vidyamala and Sona from Breathworks. There I was introduced to a whole new dimension of mindfulness. That Mindfulness is greater than awareness; that 'Mindfulness is Love.' In 2014 I embarked on professional training with Breathworks Mindfulness I began to understand that self-care isn't found in massages and chocolate cake alone but in tackling the tough stuff. I won't hide that at times this journey was tough. I experienced waves of emotion, times when I felt lost and times when I tried to run away. But the longer I stayed on the path, the more I began to feel inner peace and joy. Mindfulness brought awareness to my situations and compassion gave me the strength, courage, and responsibility to take positive action from a place of great kindness.

I took the first steps to address my debt. I sold my car, which I never drove! I cut back my spending and sought the advice and support of a financial advisor. I started to take responsibility for my happiness. I stopped all the 'fake' makeovers and ditched the toxic dating. I felt free from the pressure that these things had created in my life, to be someone I wasn't deep down. My health improved, I started to sleep better, my blood pressure stabilized and then decreased to normal levels. My menopausal symptoms faded away, maybe that would have happened anyway, but somewhere deep down I have a strong belief that my mindfulness practice supported me to accept and love myself. That in turn, this self-compassion lessened the hold of the symptoms on my life.

In 2017 I took the brave step to resign my job, albeit rather dramatically, and to devote myself to working fully in my mindfulness business. I also left Australia and came home to my roots in Sweden. Today I am thriving much of the time.

As Maya Angelo's wonderful quote goes:

'My mission in life is not merely to survive, but to thrive; and do so with some passion, some compassion, some humor, and some style.'

...Sounds like a wonderful recipe for me!

I wrote this book because I have a great passion for mindfulness. One that I believe every woman should have the opportunity to experience and bring into their life. And had I understood more about the menopause I might well have sought more information and support during this period. Although life chucked the shit bucket at me all in one go and my stress levels were high, the effects of the menopause compounded the situation. Mindfulness for me is learning to meet and live with life's challenges, to go with the flow and to simultaneously let in the good. Living that way has brought me to a very different place.

I have written this book to help you discover how mindfulness can physically, mentally and emotionally support you to discover how to calmly know the change that is occurring as you go through the menopause. To see how mindfulness can support you to heal and transform. I am deeply honored to share this book with you and hope you will find something good in it for yourself. There is no rush to read through it and know it all. The skills you can learn here will serve you all your life.

# CHAPTER 1

# THIS IS THE MENOPAUSE

*Allow*
*There is no controlling life.*
*Try corralling a lightning bolt, containing a tornado.*
*Dam a stream and it will create a new channel.*
*Resist, and the tide will sweep you off your feet.*
*Allow, and the grace will carry you to higher ground.*
*The only safety lies in letting it all in*
*The wild and the weak;*
*Fears, fantasies, failures, and success.*
*When loss rips off the door of the heart,*
*Alternatively, sadness veils your vision with despair,*
*Practice becomes merely bearing the truth.*
*In the choice to let go of your known way of being,*
*The entire world is revealed to your new eyes*

*Danna Faulds[1]*

## Chapter 1:1 The Menopause Explained

I look in the mirror. I'm looking for them, one more wrinkle, one new grey hair, checking my body for signs of sagging, the belly fat. Of course, I see that because I'm looking for it.

Where's the girl who was here yesterday? And the reply? "She's here's, but today she's better than she was yesterday."

The girl that I once was is gone. Today, I'm a stronger, smarter, wiser version.

'The Change' It comes to all us regardless of whether we're ready for it or want to happen. It is a time of rebirth and choices.

How we choose to approach the menopause will determine how we deal with the experience. If we decide to be overwhelmed or try to ignore it, we'll go through this change with little grace and almost no joy. A limiting choice. The autopilot way is not the only way. Believing that there is another way will open possibilities.

Menopause is something we've lived with from the beginning of time. Once I gave up thinking that the menopause was the end of my life. And saw it instead as a turning point what followed was liberating. Because midlife is not a time to fade into invisibility but a time to reinvent and restart. I've come to understand that the past no longer has the power to determine how I live my today or my future. I've learned to live in the present moment. Knowing that I can choose how I respond to every situation with awareness and kindness. This is mindfulness, and it can transform our experience of the menopause.

In factual terms, the menopause is when you have stopped having periods for a total of 12 months. For most women, this occurs between 45 and 55 but it can start much earlier and end later, it's very individual. Hormonal changes cause the menopause. When your body is fertile, estrogen and progesterone keep your menstrual cycle regular. But as you age, your body gradually produces less estrogen. This change in hormone levels is called the perimenopause.

The menopause is a natural and a life stage that every woman experience. Moreover, each woman's experience of the menopause is unique. Some will only have symptoms for a few months while others can continue to suffer for many years. Even after their periods have ceased. Around 80% of women experience menopausal symptoms that interfere with the quality of their life. Approximately 25% of women describe their symptoms as being severe. 10% of women must give up work due to the menopause.

Symptoms of the menopause can have a very adverse effect on you, your family and your work. It is common for symptoms to fluctuate so you may have times where you feel OK. And then other times you experience unpleasant symptoms which adversely affect the quality of your life.

There are over 34 common symptoms of menopause, some of which are familiar to women. Is it hot in here or is it only me? This is the cry of so many of my friends and family members. But not every woman has hot flushes. Every woman's experience is different. There can be vaginal dryness and fatigue due to the natural decline in estrogen. Increasingly we are beginning to recognize the mental changes that women can experience during this time. Many of the women I've interviewed speak of 'brain fog,' anxiety, and mood swings. Fortunately, all symptoms are manageable through natural and medical treatments and by adopting lifestyle changes.

Like many women, I didn't know there was a difference between perimenopause and menopause. So, what is it? Perimenopause precedes the menopause, and it usually lasts on average four years. However, it can last for up to 10 years and often begins in your 40s, but as with most aspects of the menopause, there are no set rules on the exact age.

Perimenopausal symptoms are often attributed to stress or another health condition without realizing you are menopausal. Perimenopause can be challenging to diagnose. The menopause can be confirmed by testing for low hormone levels. However, in the first few years of perimenopause, your hormone levels fluctuate, which makes diagnosis hard. Perimenopause can be a time of painful and uncomfortable symptoms. Moreover, because diagnosis can be tricky, many perimenopausal women are not given HRT (Hormone Replacement Therapy) or other treatment for their symptoms.

The estrogen levels fluctuate during the perimenopause, which can lead to a range of physical and emotional symptoms. One of the most common is irregular periods, where your menstrual cycles may lengthen or shorten. It is not only shorter, lighter periods as I know from my own experience. But that your periods can become more cumbersome, longer, late, early or even skipped! It can fluctuate and be different every month, and if you have PMS, the symptoms can worsen.

With all these changes, some of which can be unpleasant and even frightening, it isn't surprising that the menopause and perimenopause are viewed negatively by many women. 'The dreaded change' as it's called and spoken about in derogatory terms. The stigma of the menopause is very real for many women. There are the associations between hysteria and incompetence that stem from the 19th century.

These negative connotations can lead many women to approach this phase in their life stoically and not seek help. For others, the stigma can become internalized so that other people's reactions to their menopausal symptoms such as hot flushes can be unduly adverse.

However, of course, it's not all bad. The menopause can see us freed from PMS. We can experience the disappearance of health issues like asthma and endometriosis. And even a greater sense of energy and wellbeing.

I through my journey, at the same time, as I was deepening my mindfulness practice. This helped me to become more aware of my body's natural intelligence. I started paying more attention to my body's subtle signals. I was learning to pause and listen to the 'conversation' my body was having with me. Moreover, the most important lesson for me was to begin to learn what self-care and self-love are. I started to recognize, respect and nurture the fragility and beauty of my essence as a woman.

Like so many women I spent my adult life developing a busy career. Becoming a mother and doing what I thought was the 'right thing.' Often for other people and not always aligned with my values and purpose. I had until then neglected myself except for the odd day here and there. I've learned that my body isn't a machine to get me through life. But that's how I treated it, pushing, driving, overextending and compromising it. Bodies need care. They have natural cycles and rhythms and innate intelligence that can tell us a lot about ourselves and our experiences.

During perimenopause, things do start to happen that can serve as an invaluable signpost. We may begin to feel more in touch with things that have been overlooked or suppressed in our menstrual years.

Menopause and Mindfulness together gave me an opportunity to stop compromising the way I lived. And this inspired me to write this book. I believe that the changes in our bodies allow an opportunity to re-evaluate who we are. And to allow us to enter a great stage of wisdom, especially if we can cultivate more kindness towards ourselves.

Many women I've interviewed want more support going through menopause. They want reliable information. They want more discussion about what can be done to support women like themselves through menopause. Especially if they have troublesome symptoms which can leave them feeling lonely. My message is they do not have to suffer in silence.

That is why I have written this book. You are not alone! Join me as we explore the menopause with curiosity and compassion. We are all walking each other home.

## Chapter 1:2 The World Has Changed, and So Have We Women

In our mothers and our grandmother's time, the menopause signaled a slide into invisibility. And possibly the last chapter of their lives. At best they would become matronly. But more often they went grey, pulled on the 'granny pants. And became non-sexual semi-invisible beings who baked, went to local church meetings and spent time caring for their husbands and grandchildren. If they had a job outside of the home, they were a few years off retirement. After all, 60 was retirement age, and life expectancy for many was 70. Today the average life expectancy for a woman in a developed country is around 80. And we all know women who are going strong in their 90's and beyond.

I was fortunate to have two role models in my life who broke that mold. One was my grandmother, widowed in her early 50's she had no choice but to resume a career and support her family. Once she started, she didn't seem to want to stop ending up enrolling in a computer course at the local university on her 70th birthday. The other formidable woman in my family was Ursula Blackwell. A doctor who never married. She drove until she was in her 90's, traveled the world alone and ended up emigrating to Canada at 95 to live with a relative. Strong, independent women are often labeled by society as 'difficult.' I aspire to be like them!

In today's world more, women are working more than ever before. In the UK and the US, the latest figures show 70% are in gainful employment. While in my home country of Sweden close to 84% of women work.

Moreover, women nowadays work until they well into their late sixties. Indeed, the most significant increase in employment has been amongst women of 50 and over. This is for a variety of reasons, including an aging population. Employers' efforts to keep skilled workers and increases in the pension age from 60 to 65. This is likely to increase further. Many countries are suggesting that pensionable age for men and women should be 70. Even today 30% of women between the ages of 65 -69 are working, up from 15% in the late 1980's.

The average age of menopause is 51, so many more women are experiencing this while in employment. Compared to pregnancy and maternity, menopause is not well understood or catered for in workplaces. The women I have interviewed who worked have found symptoms, especially hot flushes, challenging to manage. And work with all its stresses can even exacerbate these symptoms. Something I know all too well.

Taboos about revealing menopausal symptoms at work are real. Only half of the women who take time off from work, due to menopausal symptoms, disclose the reason for their absence. Some women don't want to admit they are going through it. Men don't want to talk about "women issues. Many managers and colleagues are unaware of the workplace impact of the menopause until they know someone is going through menopause. Or, they are experiencing it themselves. There are inherent sexism and biases built into organizations that disadvantage women. Although we can talk about breast cancer and pregnancy, the menopause is a subject that is rarely addressed. 20% of women surveyed by the British Occupational Health Research Foundation[2] believe that menopause has had a negative impact on their managers and colleagues' perceptions of their competence.

Due to many changes in our society women in their 40; s and early 50's finds they are juggling caring responsibilities with holding down paid employment. Running a household still falls to women. Even in gender-equal Sweden, 60% of home duties are done by women.

Many of us have delayed motherhood due to careers and the advent of IVF until the late 30's or later. I was 37 when my son was born, and I have several friends who have been in their early 40's when they have their first child. This means we are often becoming perimenopausal as our children hit the moody teenager stage. Emotions in households can run high as I well know. The arguments, the door slamming, shouting and swearing all down to hormones! At times my son Thomas would roll his eyes at me and say' Why are you so angry all the time?'. I would deny I was angry and put down my outbursts to the work-related stress. Or the financial pressures of being a single mother and a million other reasons.

For our generation, this is the new norm. Any woman giving birth while in her 30s will experience her perimenopause alongside her children's puberty. Also, we have limited role models. Many of us never see our own mothers' menopause. Women gave birth in their twenties and would have been mid-thirties when their children reached puberty. When they hit perimenopause, their children were grown up.

Moreover, then the often-unspoken extra responsibility - our parents. We become what is being termed "Sandwich Generation

Caregivers'. The average profile of a caregiver is a woman 48- to 59-years-old, according to the and menopause spans ages 45 to 55. Both life passages are recent, and so the bonus of longevity in our modern era includes these twin challenges. One out of eight Americans between the ages of 40 to 60 is playing a juggling act between the younger and older generations[3]. That number is rising as baby boomers reach retirement age and life expectancy increases.

This is not a new phenomenon to care for your parents. But the fact that families are smaller than they once and there is, in general, less social capital means there is less family support to share the burden.

The stress of caregiving and menopause is a "vicious cycle" that can exacerbate menopausal symptoms and can impact a caregiver's overall health and ability to care for their loved one. Caregiver burnout is rampant, and even though you don't live with your parent, you may have to provide household or financial help or run errands for your aging parents.

It's happening all around me. A close friend of mind, an only child, was close to burning out from being the sole caretaker for her 80-year-old mother on top of running a business and being a single parent. Another complained that her parents were becoming more and more demanding. And she found that she was spending a significant part of her time researching assisted living facilities.

So, is it any wonder that so many of us feel tired and emotional?

With all the challenges of work, children, our parents and our raging hormones we need to find balance. A way to deal with life in a more focused, compassionate way. Enter stage left: Mindfulness.

## Chapter 1:3 What is Mindfulness

It is entirely possible that you've heard or read something about mindfulness. It has grown in popularity in recent years, with more people attending mindfulness training. But, what is mindfulness? I like this definition of mindfulness:

"Mindfulness means paying attention to purpose, non-judgmentally in the present moment with curiosity and kindness so we can choose our behavior in line with our values."

The best way to understand mindfulness is to experience it. So here is a mini-mindfulness exercise.

*Get yourself into a comfortable position, sitting or lying down. Relax and allow yourself to settle.*

*Bring awareness to what are you doing and thinking at this moment. What are you experiencing right now? What are you doing right now? What thoughts are passing through your mind? Notice the thoughts that come up and acknowledge them but let them pass. Can you look AT your thoughts, not from them? Tune yourself into the present moment.*

*Now take a moment to bring your attention to your breathing for six breaths. Focus attention on one thing: your breath. Be aware of the movement of your body with each breath. Of how your chest rises and falls, how your belly pushes in and out, and how your lungs expand and contract. Find the pattern of your breath and anchor yourself to the present with this awareness.*

*Expand your awareness outward, first to the body then to the environment. Allow the awareness to expand out to your body. How does your body feel? Notice the sensations you are experiencing, like tightness, aches, or lightness in your face or shoulders. Be open to any sensations with an attitude of kindly curiosity.*

*If you wish, you can then expand your awareness even further to the environment around you. Bring your attention to what is in front of you. Notice the colors, shapes, patterns, and textures of the objects you can see. Be present at this moment, in your awareness of your surroundings.*

*"When you are ready to finish the exercise, allow your eyes to open and try to carry that mindfulness with you as you go about your day."*

Mindfulness involves paying attention "on purpose." It is a conscious direction of our awareness. "mindfulness" and "awareness" are not interchangeable. I may be aware that I'm irritable, but that wouldn't mean I was mindful of my irritability. To be mindful, I must be aware of myself, not just vaguely and habitually aware[4].

Most of us are aware of what we're doing, but we're thinking about hundreds of other things at the same time, scanning social media, talking, or reading or even all these and many more! Because we are only partially aware of our thoughts, they wander. There's no conscious attempt to bring our attention back to here and now. Our to-do lists and thoughts continuously drive us. "What do I need to do today?" Moreover, we develop the habit of getting lost in the stories in our heads. Ruminating about past events and planning for the future.

The significant part of mindfulness is that our awareness is intentional. It means staying with our experience, whether that's the breath, or an emotion Or something as simple as walking or showering. This deliberate awareness means that we are shaping our minds. By intentionally directing our awareness towards our present moment experiences, we decrease their effect on our lives. And we create space which in turn leads us to feel calmer.

Left to itself the mind goes through all kinds of thoughts. Ruminating about past event or dreaming about the futures. We have a natural tendency to negativity. It's part of our survival mechanism. Many of our thoughts are negative and can include anger, craving, revenge or self-pity. When we indulge in these kinds of thoughts, we reinforce those emotions and cause ourselves to suffer. This continuous stream of thinking means that we believe our thoughts to be real. We overlook and disregard the endless possibility and power of the present moment. It's exhausting.

Cognitively, mindfulness is the awareness that there experiences that are pleasant. And some are unpleasant, but on an emotional level, we don't react. We learn not judge that this experience is good or bad. Alternatively, if we do make those judgments, we learn to notice them, acknowledge them and let go of them. We don't get upset because we're experiencing something we don't want to be happening. We accept whatever arises.

Whether it's a pleasant or a painful we treat it the same way. We cultivate an inner calm and balance of mind.

Sounds amazing right? But, a bit hard. The good news is that mindfulness is an innate capacity to be aware here and now, a natural ability we all have. Watch any child playing, see how absorbed and at the moment, they are. As adults, we've lost that innate capacity. Mindfulness can help us recapture this ability.

How do we become more mindful especially during the menopause? At a time in our lives when the mind and body seem to have taken on a life of their own. Many women going through the menopause come to mindfulness with a need to switch off the mind chatter. Or at least learn how to get a break from that constant stream of dialogue. That has been my own experience. I came to mindfulness during peri-menopause which coincided with some dramatic changes in my work life. I was stressed, and as I now know, menopause can make things worse. My biggest fear was burnout and becoming unable to continue working. This created massive pressure as I was a single mother and my son was only 14 at the time.

I stumbled upon mindfulness by accident in 2013. After connecting with an amazing woman whose calmness and sense of presence blew me away. I followed up with Heather and discovered she was an accredited mindfulness teacher. The organization she worked for had a training center near my house, and so the journey began. It started with that an 8-week MBSR (mindfulness-based stress reduction course). Healing my fractured mind, calming and centering me. And giving me a perspective on my stressful job situation, though it took me another four years to resolve that situation. The experience set me on a path to becoming a mindfulness coach. To help other women to transform through the simple and powerful act of being more present and accepting of their situation.

As Eckhart Tolle said, "When you are in the present moment, you break the continuity of your story, of past and present. Then true intelligence arises, and love."[5]

Mindfulness is about being aware of what we're doing while we're doing it. Noticing our thinking, feeling our feelings arising as they are in the present moment. This quality of awareness means that we feel kindness, curiosity, openness, and acceptance. We can perceive with all our senses. And this takes our attention away from the stream of thoughts in our heads. We can open to recognizing that we are more than our thoughts, more than our feelings.

Mindfulness is our innate ability to be aware of and hold thoughts, feelings, sounds, body sensations, without the need for these to drive our actions all the time. We step back. We observe reality as it is, no more, no less. We see how our mind's habit of creating stories makes us stressed when our expectations aren't met. When we're mindful; we're less reactive. We accept reality as it is.

Mindfulness can lead to less stress, worry, negativity. And replace that with better focus, better productivity, better sleep. That means that there is the possibility of greater well-being, enjoyment, and happiness.

Research is showing that practicing mindfulness can help our bodies feel healthier by boosting our immune systems and that we have more positive emotional states. We gain a profound sense of self-awareness and self-compassion, and that leads to happiness.[6]

With all these benefits mindfulness makes sense for the menopause. The benefits to our mental and physical health when we are present to live mindfully, when we've got over the noise in our heads, and experience life more deeply, are enormous. We see the trivial things we tend to ignore aren't small after all. We can see trees in bloom, the warmth of a hug, smiles. We notice and savor the most ordinary moments of each day, precious moments that make up our whole life.

It's becoming clear how mindfulness can be applied to the menopause, the menopause with all its raging emotions, thoughts, and body sensations. It can teach us that, well, you're just here, just now. That we are often unable always to control what's going on. But so noticing and accepting, our wild thoughts are that thoughts, not facts help us to feel calm and in control

## Chapter 1:4 How Can Mindfulness Support Us Through the Menopause?

Mindfulness has excellent benefits for those of us who are struggling with the physical and emotional ups and downs of the menopause. We're aware that menopause can create emotional issues. Hormonal surges and plunges accompanied by concerns that we're losing our youth and vitality. It's a potent mix. We can hardly blame ourselves for responding negatively.

I know some women sail through the menopause. But, for most of us, there is a bit more of an emotional rollercoaster. Mindfulness may help women to get through our emotional ups and downs.

We know that the action of the menopausal hormones on mood is complex. The hormonal imbalance in women during perimenopause and menopause itself leads women to experience higher levels of stress. Estrogen, a female sex hormone, helps manage the level of cortisol in the body. When this hormone starts to drop during the menopause, a woman's body has less capacity to normalize the surges in cortisol levels. This condition causes women to experience more stress during the menopause. We can find ourselves in a vicious cycle. The more anxious we become, the more stressed we become, the more cortisol is released, and so it goes. To supply adequate amounts of cortisol, doctors may advise their menopausal patients to undergo hormonal therapy such as hormone replacement therapy. However, mindfulness also helps.

You can't, of course, practice mindfulness to alter your estrogen levels. But you can take control of the cortisol. By practicing mindfulness, we can reduce the rate at which cortisol is released into the body. Lower cortisol means our fight or flight mechanism is dialed down. The reduction of stress and anxiety due to lower cortisol levels lead to better sleep. Something every one of us could do with more. Especially if night sweats and feelings of anxiety are disrupting your zzz's. Moreover, recent findings show that mindfulness can make the brain more resilient to life changes. A study by the Scientific American revealed that an eight-week mindfulness course was able to reduce the size of the amygdala, the part of the brain linked to fear and emotions. While the brain's prefrontal cortex, the section associated with awareness, focus, and decision making, thickens. Mindfulness remodels the brain to make it more resilient to stress.

It isn't just me, a passionate advocate for mindfulness talking. Scientific studies support what many of us have known that mindfulness works for the menopause. There have been many studies of the benefits of mindfulness on the menopause. The University of Massachusetts study showed that women experienced a reduction of up to 40% in the number of hot flashes after taking a mindfulness course. Moreover, in some studies, women have reported that they're less bothered by their symptoms. They have a greater sense of wellbeing. Mindfulness doesn't remove the symptoms of menopause, but it does help you to deal with them more calmly and compassionately. And there is unmistakable evidence that self-compassion improves our mental and physical wellbeing. Practicing mindfulness gives us an ability to focus our awareness on the present moment, to relax the body and ride out the storm that occurs. Mindfulness can be highly beneficial whether our reaction is physical like a hot flash or a mood rising.

Menopause is a process. Moreover, what works at one stage may not work at the next. Mindfulness means accepting without judgment. Allowing what is happening, and being able, even for a moment, to acknowledge and accept can give us a sense of distance and perspective. This helps a lot as the menopause fluctuates our moods and body sensations. By practicing mindfulness, we are allowing a lot of the menopause symptoms to be there. This behavior leads to a greater sense of relaxation and well-being. It gives us the ability to step out of the negative thinking that spirals us downwards. This sense of perspective helps us to foster greater self-compassion and more joy and appreciation of life even when we're feeling less than great.

The benefits of mindfulness for the menopause are:

1. Mindfulness will help you cope with the stress of the menopause. On a day to day basis observing and dealing with the different sensations, emotions, and thoughts that arise during this time. Moreover, mindfulness will help you better deal with the future-anxiety that such a momentous change brings to your life

2. Mindfulness will help you gain perspective on the changes that unfold as the menopause progresses. You can let go of thinking of how things ought to be. And allow this stage of your life to unfold year on year, experience after experience, with more kindness and compassion towards yourself.

But, isn't mindfulness just meditation? That's a question I get quite often. Moreover, to some extent that's true. You could become mindful without any meditating, but it would be harder. Mindfulness is a skill and meditation is the tool that helps gets you to cultivate that skill. When you set aside time for reflection, you're helping to train your heart and mind to be focused and positive.

Moreover, like any practice the more you do it, the better you become. Same as learning a language or laying an instrument. What you put in you get back and although it might seem like a chore. But the benefits of doing a mindfulness practice far outweigh the 15 to 20 minutes a day. And that's all that's needed to feel the positive effects.

Three central meditation approaches that will form that basis of the mindfulness meditation practices in this book.

This is the first step in learning to gain some control over our monkey minds. It's bringing back our attention to one focal point repeatedly. This could be the breath, sounds around you or a specific object like a candle flame or a mantra. Of these, the breath is the most commonly used method. It is free. And the breath teaches us about flow and the changing nature of our experiences as no two breaths are the same.

## Open Monitoring

Once you have begun to master focused awareness you can start investigating monitoring is another type of meditation called open monitoring. In contrast to Focused Awareness, there is no object or event in the internal or external environment that the meditator must focus on. The aim is rather to stay in the monitoring state, attentive to any experience that might arise, without selecting, judging, or focusing on any specific object. It's like viewing your experience through a wide-angle lens. Letting feelings, emotions, sensations, and thoughts come and go. It helps to make you feel calmer, balanced, more open and able to gain perspective on any given situation.

## Loving Kindness

The third main type of meditation is Loving-kindness meditation which incorporates elements of both focused awareness and open monitoring. This is a scientifically proven practice that helps to build positive emotions and builds resilience. Scientific studies have shown that practicing this meditation can alter your self-confidence and self-worth. And we need a boost in these areas during the menopause years. It helps to calm your emotions and impact positively on your physical health.

During this meditation, you focus on developing love and compassion first for yourself. And then extend this love to ever more others (e.g., from self to a friend, to someone one does not know, to all living beings. Any negative associations that might arise are replaced by positive ones.

These types of meditation provide a path to coping better with the onset and development of the menopause. Moreover, the real beauty is how simple and accessible they are.

At each stage in this book, there will be ways that you develop your innate capacity to be mindful. This will help you better manage the various challenges that will arise step by step. Working with some of the suggested practices can help you navigate the ups and downs of this stage in our lives. From the perimenopause, through the endless years of change and raging hormones. And then how mindfulness can help us step into the new and exciting phase of post menopause.

We're going to start with our bodies. Learning how mindfulness can calm, accept and love our bodies as they change through this stage of our lives.

## In Summary

- The menopause is an inevitable life transition for women. It typically occurs in our later 40's and early 50's and lasts for several years. But every woman's experience is unique. Menopause doesn't have a positive image in Western culture and is often associated with physical, mental and emotional difficulties. And indeed there are over 34 common symptoms of menopause, some of which are familiar to women. But many are less well known. Fortunately, all symptoms are manageable through natural and medical treatments and by adopting lifestyle changes.
- Mindfulness involves paying attention "on purpose." It is a conscious direction of our awareness to our present moment experience that could be our breath, or an emo-

tion Or something as simple as walking or showering. By intentionally directing our awareness towards our present moment experiences, we decrease their effect on our lives. And we create space which in turn leads us to feel calmer, more positive and happier.

- Mindfulness can lead to less stress, less worry, and negativity. And replace that with better focus, better productivity, better sleep. That means that there is the possibility of greater well-being, enjoyment, and happiness. No wonder more and more health practitioners are advocating mindfulness to help us through the menopause with all its raging emotions, thoughts, and body sensations. It can teach us that, well, you're just here, just now and that everything is OK just as it is. And that nothing stays the same, everything is in a state of flow and will change. That gives us hope.

# CHAPTER 2

# LISTENING TO THE BODY

*Listen to the fragile feelings*
*Not to the clashing fury*
*To the quiet sounds*
*Not to the loud clamor*
*To the steady heartbeat*
*Not to the noisy confusion*
*To the hidden voices*
*Not to the obvious chatter*
*To the deep harmonies*
*Not to the surface discord*

(found on the wall of a church in The Forest Bowland, UK)

## Chapter 2.1 Connecting with the Changing Body

Overheated, I'm turning redder and redder by the minute. My face, neck, décolletage, looking like a severe case of sunburn or an overcooked tomato. Moreover, then the sweat, I can feel it running down my back. Also, my mind goes blank because all I can feel are these body sensations. Standing up to give a presentation in front of my CEO and I'm a mess. A hot mess, and not in the right way! I'm embarrassed, anxious and I concerned that I appear incompetent. Moreover, the loneliness. Who I'm going to confide in? That my rushed, awkward presentation was due to the menopause creating havoc? No one. Worst still is the nagging concern that I smell because of all the sweating. Our overactive hypothalamus due to lower estrogen tricks us into sweating more. And, no one at work ever knows how to approach the subject of body odor.

The sad thing is that I was not alone in feeling this way. Many of the women I interviewed have felt the same. Women can suffer throughout the menopause. Our bodies change so much, and we're not ready for it. It's the unpreparedness and the speed at which the body reacts that rocks us. So many women have said I wish there had been more information.

All sorts of strange things start happening to us. We become best friends with our tweezers as hair sprouts in all directions. We've got minor bumps that turn into massive bruises, and sometimes our eyes water for no reason.

All those things are part of our changing hormonal status. Moreover, physical symptoms, of the menopause, are many and complicated for us to live with. Visible signs can cause considerable stress. The unwanted hair or alopecia. The hair on our body goes, and that's a positive, and instead pops up on our face. We need to go to the toilet all the time, and we don't do jumping jacks without some trepidation.

Moreover, the sudden speed and irregularity of our heart can be quite scary. I would feel like my heart was racing at a hundred miles an hour. Epinephrine and norepinephrine, neurotransmitters that regulate our heart rate and blood pressure fluctuate. Many women talked about waking up from night sweats, feeling as if their hearts were in their mouths.

Moreover, then the thing we don't talk about, sex. Here in Sweden, we talk about vaginal dryness on TV ads. But not all the pain and suffering this causes. It's like your vagina's a desert, your skin, and your eyes as well. You're like this dried up thing, and with this dryness, we get painful sex and even itching. A friend of my families had such lousy itch; she had to rush into doorways when in town and scratch herself. Unfortunately, her doctor's diagnosis was that she hadn't had enough children. Hm, given that she'd birthed eight children, that comment was way off the mark.

It's not easy to love yourself, the woman you were is no longer here. We can never reclaim our 20-something body. But, we can take hold of our present emotional and physical wellbeing. We must appreciate and care for the bodies that we have now.

For some of us, that's are quite hard because we live in a world that's youth-obsessed. Daily we see images of slim young women. Beautiful people. Moreover, even if there have been some steps to use older models. It's still tokenism. Marketing roles and advertising agencies are the domain of millennials. So, the youthful images dominate. And it's easy to become obsessed about our bodies, our weight, our shape, during the menopause because it's in opposition to societal standards.

Believe you me; we won't be thin like we're before the menopause. It is likely that you will put on weight, particularly around the middle. On average, a woman between 45 and 55 gains a half a kilo a year. Moreover, its abdominal fat that's associated with our hormonal changes. Although things like HRT can reverse some of the development of abdominal fat, it's not that easy.

We can become very frustrated when social media's trying to tell us that we should have a diet. We should look this way, feel this way and it doesn't work when we're going through the menopause.

Sometimes we'd like to run away from the menopause, but we can't. The constant hot flashes, the dryness, the thin skin, the weight, makes us feel brittle. We can develop blocking behaviors like plastic surgery and Botox. Over-exercising or that extra glass of wine. Crazy diets.

We can be angry, irritable, as we can push against the unpleasant sensations. One of the women whom I interviewed, had hardened. Her attitude was, "No! The menopause is nothing! Get on with it. Stop talking about; it is a first world issue,". An indulgence. There was hardening against the unpleasant sensations. There was an over-stoicism.

While other women are completely overwhelmed, they can lack interest in life, and they feel exhausted. And these feelings can lead to self-pitying, feelings of dullness and passivity and a loss of wanting to take the initiative in any aspect of their lives. Leaving women feeling lost and withdrawn, preoccupied and lonely, anxious and even depressed. Moreover, many women are moving between blocking behaviors, like indulging into too much alcohol, chocolate, shopping to name but a few. Or drowning behaviors, where lying on the couch, shutting out life is all they want to do.

The menopause is an unavoidable fact of life. Even though HRT and other medication can help, they should be a choice not a given. If we try to banish our body changes we're setting ourselves up for much unhappiness.

So, what can we do?' Mindfulness teaches us to accept things as they are. It shows us to stop resisting the changes that many of us don't like. To change how we relate to our body and the uncomfortable sensations. Moment by moment.

The first stage of mindfulness is learning to come into more significant connection with our body. Learning to feel sensations in the body, both the intense and subtle ones. We're tuning in to our inner sense now. We learn to recognize our states of arousal early, like the hot flashes, the heart in mouth, etc. So, we can respond to them with more kindness and choice. In each moment we can always stop and breathe. Learn to explore these sensations with curiosity and non-judgment.

One straightforward exercise is to bring attention to a part of the body where you notice stress.

*What are the sensations there? How would you describe them?*

*Give yourself 2 or 3 minutes to observe the sensations without trying to change them.*

*What happens? Are they changing? How would you describe them?*

The very act of paying attention to your body brings into focus that sensations are changing and not all sensations are negative. Moreover, this is the first step in learning to calm the body.

## 2.2 Calming the Body

Calming the body is an essential part of learning to cope and live with menopause symptoms. Why start with our bodies, our hormonal, uncomfortable and even painful bodies? The body is part of who you are, and we can't alienate ourselves from it, though we may not like the changes that are going on. At best, we can become self-conscious, and at worst, we don't love our body and want to cut it loose. The more we try to pull away from our bodies and all the discomfort and changes that are happening there. The more restless and stressed we become. Even more alienated. It's a lose-lose thing. Instead of becoming more aware of our bodies and becoming more mindful of all the sensations gives us an anchor during this transition process.

Why do we need to calm the body? Menopause is stressful and made even more so because of the hormonal changes that occur during this transition period. As we know our hormonal levels, change dramatically, and this also changes the way we physically and emotionally respond to stress. We produce cortisol and adrenaline from the adrenal glands. They don't get a great press, which is a shame because they work hard to helps us cope when we experience stressful situations. Cortisol and adrenalin are our fight-flight or freeze hormones, and they also create energy, focus, and alertness so we can survive.

Pre-menopause our bodies produce progesterone in levels that work against the impact of cortisol on the body. And this means we have a natural buffer to stress. During the menopause, the adrenal glands take over some of the work of the ovaries and start to produce lesser amounts of progesterone and estrogen. The body is adapting to the transition of the menopause. But, if we're under too much stress, the adrenal glands will pump out more cortisol and adrenalin in preference to estrogen and progesterone. After all, the body will always choose survival over fertility. With the buffering capability of progesterone weakened, we are more sensitive to stress and its adverse effects. The women I've spoken to report not being able to sleep well, feeling low in energy, bloated and gaining weight around the waistline. These symptoms are linked to elevated cortisol levels in the body.

Plus, we can experience pains that can be debilitating. Vaginal atrophy, a thinning of the vaginal walls, effects 75% of women. It results in painful symptoms including burning, itching or vaginal dryness. Many women develop migraines headaches. I remember my mother living with almost 15 years of crippling migraines. She would spend days in a darkened room, and we had to tiptoe around the house. I admire how as a single mother she still held down her job in the stockbroking throughout this time. Even if she sometimes had to create the illusion of being away at a meeting. Sleeping off the worst of the attack under her desk so as not to lose her job.

Cultivating the capacity to help calm the body becomes very important during peri-menopause and menopause. As we no longer can rely on the extra support of estrogen and progester-one we need to actively and consciously learn to balance our nervous system. The autonomic nervous system controls everything in our body. Breathing, sweating, digestion and more. When we're feeling stressed the sympathetic nervous system is dominant the body goes into fight or flight mode. The other part of the autonomic nervous system is the parasympathetic nervous system. It's the counterbalance. It helps us to feel calm.

Why can't we think our way out of things? Have you ever tried to figure your way out of a hot flash? I used to try to rationalize my way out and found myself feeling heady the more analytical I became. My thoughts went in circles, out of control and even became obsessive at times. What I've now learned is that in doing this I was activating the sympathetic nervous system even more in my attempt to escape from the way I felt.

Mindfulness teaches us to come back to our direct sensory experiences. And in so doing we activate the parasympathetic nervous system. We're not so lost in our thoughts, and we can ground back into the present moment and direct sensory experiences. The more we can train ourselves to be mindfully aware of our bodies. To notice what we can feel, smell, touch, taste, hear. The more we become able to manage our unhelpful mental and emotional habits. And break create the vicious cycle of stress and anxiety that our fluctuating hormones set in motion.

One of the simplest ways is to practice grounding techniques. They help us to orientate ourselves to the here and now. They are helpful when we are overwhelmed or anxious. They help us to gain mental focus. There are two ways that I've found, both for myself and my clients that work the best.

An excellent grounding technique is to stop, look around your room. Notice your surroundings and notice the details. This the grounding exercise that I call the 54321:

*Name five things you can see in the place.*

*Name four things you could feel like feet on the floor, bum on the chair, the clothes against your skin.*

*Name three things you can hear right now, fingers tapping, music in the background, traffic.*

*Name two things you can smell right now or the things you like the smell of if there are no smells around you.*

*Then one good thing about yourself.*

Doing this at any time of the day or night can help you come back into the here and now. It stops all the racing that's going on when our minds are spinning due to cortisol circulating at elevated levels in our bodies.

The other approach is The Body Scan sometimes called Body Sensing. This is a fundamental mindfulness practice that I used daily once I discovered it. You rotate your attention throughout your physical body. And observe the physical and energetic sensations that are present.

Through practicing the body scan, you become more familiar with your body. You can feel more and more of the subtle sensations that can signal that something might crop up. The body scan helps us to come back to our bodies. We can do the practice daily or several times a day. We are learning to identify what we're feeling, where we're feeling it and releasing that stress. It helps us stay or return to a relaxed state when we become too tense.

This is an adapted version of an exercise used in Compassion Focused Therapy[1] that I particularly like for its simplicity and gentleness:

*The best way to do this is to get comfortable.*

*Sit or lie in a warm place. Then try and get into a position that is comfortable enough for you to relax without becoming so comfortable you fall asleep.*

*Let your breathing slow down. Focus on your breath until you find a sense or feel of the rhythm that is comfortable and soothing for you. If that seems hard, don't worry breathe in a way that's comfortable for you.*

*Then start to notice bring your attention to your body. Start by focusing on your legs. Notice how they feel. Do you feel any tension, tightness, pain, concentrated energy? Try to be with it for a minute and notice what you're feeling. Zone in on your uncomfortable areas. Focus on them. Breathe into them and see what happens. The imagine all that tension and discomfort flowing down into the floor and away. Imagine it floating away as you breathe in and out. Explore letting go with kindness. Imagine the gratitude your legs feel as they let go of the tension, tightness, and pain.*

*Now move down through the body, to your shoulders. Repeating the body scan steps, noticing if there's tightness, uncomfortable feelings, tension, pressure or pain. Breathe into the areas you notice. Stay with those feelings. Relax, relax. Breathe into it. As you breathe out to imagine the tension leaving the shoulders, down through the floor and away. Imagine emptying a vessel of tension and discomfort. Your body is grateful, and you feel kind towards it.*

*Continue with this, through the stomach and back. Relax, breathe and feel the tension flowing away.*

*Bring the attention to the arms, hands, and fingers. Notice any tension, pain or discomfort and imagine that it is released, out through the floor and away.*

*Finally, bring attention to the tension that sits in your head and neck. Notice how you feel, where you hold your stress, what sensations you're experiencing. Breathe, notice, relax. Release it, out through the floor.*

*Rest and focus on the whole body. Each time you breathe out to focus on the keyword RELAX for a minute or so. Imagine your body becoming more relaxed.*

*Take a deeper breath, notice how your body feels and how grateful it is to you for spending some time letting go of tension,*

It is possible that your feelings become more intense during this practice. But as they continue their scanning and keep the focus, and the feeling will dissipate. Keep your awareness on that feeling for a little while. Stay present. Continue and breathe.

This exercise can help you release tension in your body now. And when those anxious feelings or sweats, that feel so uncontrollable like they're going to engulf you, you accept and let those feelings be there without feeling the need to resist or push them away.

You may not be able to stop the physical symptoms. But you can lessen the impact of them on you, and they often aren't as intense when you practice this over time.

You can do this practice for 15 or 20 minutes. Or, you can do an abbreviated version by noticing any place in your body where you're carrying that tension. Instead of scanning from head to toe. Moving towards our physical body helps us to become more aware of the exact nature of our experience. And how it shifts over time to gaining perspective on how fluid the quality of our experience is.

## 2.3 Embracing the Changes

Many of the women I've interviewed while researching this book have felt confused and share a similar dialogue "What is going on? I'm exercising and eating healthily and doing everything right. But I'm tired, I can't think straight, I feel plagued by hot flashes, and I can't seem to lose weight around my waist." These women are not alone. Many feels discouraged by the body changes that happen as entering menopause. In searching the internet, I found many articles about how to "fight" the changes of menopause. This resistance approach is often tied up with a fantasy of going back to being young.

Recent research from the University of Cambridge has shown that a body-centric perspective might have a significant impact on how well you cope through the menopause. In a study of 270 women it that those who were more concerned with their physical appearance that tended to have more negative attitudes about menopause. Moreover, that a reduced ability to accept the menopause also resulted in more suffering from mental and physical health problems during their menopausal years.

Why the link? Our appearance tends to change during menopause. Women who've "become used to being noticed and have enjoyed the attention" struggle that with the menopause comes aging. They can come to resent this phase and feel bad about it," says the study's lead author, Dr. Helena Rubinstein, at the University of Cambridge[2].

But why struggle? Instead, choose to embrace your body as it ages. The body changes that occur during aging are not something to be feared, fought or struggled against. A fellow mindfulness teacher shared this about the uncertain and sometimes surprising changes during menopause: "Here's the thing, aging is completely normal and natural. It is something we all experience, and for many, it's something to be fortunate to experience."

It's normal that when we experience unpleasant changes, discomfort or pain that we resist and try to push away these sensations, whether they're physical, mental or emotional. Or, we can succumb to them passively accepting and even becoming overwhelmed by these inevitable changes. Either way, we are setting ourselves to fail or to suffer unnecessary distress. Many of us, myself included, have ingrained habits. So, when we experience the various changes associated with the menopause, be they hot flashes, vaginal discomfort or other body changes, we overlay these physical sensations with opinions and value judgments.

This where mindfulness can help. It can teach us to rest our awareness in the body. As described earlier, bringing objectivity to our body and it's changing nature. Mindfulness can show us how to accept things as they are without making harsh value judgments. Peeling away the distorted thinking and the reactive feelings that arise like fear, anxiety, anger or frustration.

An important part of mindfulness is understanding that what we resist, persists. Practicing mindfulness teaches us how to strip away all the layers of resistance. In doing mindfulness practices like the body scan, we can explore and approach our bodies. We can open and examine 'the discomfort, the pain' with curiosity and kindness. By practicing acceptance in this way, we are interrupting the production of stress hormones in the body and this in turn, helps to reduce any physical or emotional or mental pain. We can begin to see that body sensation have impermanence to them. Even checking out the most intense feelings, the hottest hot flash, the burning, the itching even the migraine, we can see these are not as fixed and solid as we imagine. They are in fact fluid and changing moment by moment. Opening our awareness of the smallest shift is an excellent place to start.

I find the description of how to embrace what's going on from the American psychologist and self-compassion expert Dr. Christopher Germer[3] particularly useful. This approach describes acceptance as having four distinct stages. These help us to work with this sometimes-difficult concept of not trying to escape from the unpleasant and unwanted experiences of the menopause. Moreover, slowly working through this process, not advancing to the next stage before being comfortable with where you are in the moment. The four steps are:

1. Aversion - resistance, over-thinking, avoidance
2. Curiosity - turn to our situation with interest
3. Tolerance - stoic acceptance
4. Allowing - letting things come and go, see the fluid nature of our body's reactions

Friendship - see hidden value in the menopause

Our instinctive reaction to any discomfort, pain or unpleasantness is to want to push it away, to try to figure out how to remove it. With the menopause, this approach doesn't work. We can't think our way out of this or reverse these changes. And doing so creates mental anguish and in turn, can make our symptoms even worse.

If we practice acceptance, we then move to the second stage of 'Curiosity.' We can ask ourselves some questions like 'What am I feeling?'. We can get granular about the situations under which symptoms seem acuter 'When does this happen'? Asking these questions will provide some insight into the ways we could better manage our days to minimize the effects. We usually try the third stage 'Tolerance.' The stoic acceptance of the menopause that I've encountered in so many women. The 'enduring' of the unpleasantness.

We can find our resistance starts to disappear during 'Allow" and we can see that painful and uncomfortable feelings in our body come and go on their own. Moreover, finally, as we adapt, we may even see value in the menopause. We are entering a new phase for our bodies; we will be freed from monthly periods and the need for contraception. All this can be very liberating.

That's not to say that opening in this way isn't a challenge. If our body sensations are intense, it can be challenging to bring acceptance and curiosity to these sensations. If we begin and practice, we can change our relationship to with our changing body. We can feel more connected and whole and able to live a valued life. Mindfulness can help us to be able to transform any moment where we feel like victim into a moment of the initiative.

A final word on acceptance is to remember it's not about tolerating extreme discomfort or pain. It's about opening to what's happening within in us now, acknowledging the situation. Acceptance isn't resignation when we accept with awareness.

## 2.4 Learning to Love Your Body

Becoming kind to yourself is very, very important. Embracing your body and its aging process is not something to fear, fight or struggle with. It can be uncertain and surprising, but it is healthy and natural. Self-kindness, wanting kindness or even making every effort to be kind and gentle to oneself is natural. Many women I work with can see this is a weakness or an indulgence. They believe they don't deserve it.

Bringing a kind gentle attitude towards the changing body can take a while. However, the critical thing here is your intention and desire to love your body. It may take a while before your feelings follow. Your purpose and efforts to become compassionate are what counts. There is now much evidence that self-kindness is associated with well-being. And being able to cope with life's stresses.

If you're suffering through hot flashes (or any other symptom), relief might be closer than you think. According to a study, women who practiced self-compassion were less likely to report that hot flashes are interfering with their lives and messing with their moods. Australian researchers questioned women (aged 40 to 60) who were experiencing the tell-tale menopauses symptoms. and measured their levels of self-compassion through questions like, "When I see aspects of my personality that I don't like, I get down on myself." They found that those rated higher on self-compassion reported that their symptoms interfered less with their daily lives than women who demonstrated lower levels of kindness towards themselves.

So how exactly does being kind to yourself make the experience of hot flashes different? "Hot flushes and night sweats can trigger challenging thoughts and emotions that contribute to making the experience more negative," says Lydia Brown, from the University of Melbourne[4]. "If a woman wakes up sweating, she may feel irritated because her sleep is interrupted. And anxious that she might not feel refreshed in the morning. These types of thoughts prolong the experience and make falling back to sleep more difficult."

Resisting the urge to get frustrated when a hot flash strikes are easier said than done. However, the principle behind it is simple. "Self-compassion involves responding to one's suffering with the same tenderness as one would give to a child or loved one who is hurt," says Brown. One suggestion is to place a hand on your heart area when you feel the heat hit. And then thinking about a loved one to put yourself in the right headspace. "Speaking to ourselves in friendly emotional ways paired with self-accepting thoughts are powerful strategies to ease the burden of menopause symptoms including hot flashes and night sweats.". Of course, this approach can be well applied to other menopausal conditions.

Another fantastic way that helps to build a kinder and more caring attitude towards our menopausal bodies are focused on compassion exercises. These are designed to try and create feelings to stimulate our soothing systems in some way and to help us learn to be kind and supportive, to ourselves. And to send us helpful messages when things are hard for us. We are more likely to stimulate those parts of our brain that respond to kindness, and in turn, this will help us cope with the stress and the changes occurring in the body during this whole period of transformation.

This because these feelings of soothing from a place of kindness help us to feel safe. Substances in our brain called endorphins are essential for feeling calm and wellbeing. These are also released when we feel kindness. There is also a hormone called oxytocin, which links to our feelings of social safeness and affiliation. This hormone (along with the endorphins) gives us feelings of well-being.

One approach you can try is to can explore for yourself what contentedness or kindness is like by remembering what your body feels like when you are content. Or when others have been kind to you or when you think kindly towards yourself. When you feel safe and content, what do you attend and think about? How do you behave when you're safe and satisfied?

Alternatively, you can try this exercise of creating a safe internal space, which Dr. Richard Miller, founder of iRest Yoga Nidra likes to call an Inner Resource[5]. This is a tool that can help you feel secure, at ease and in control of your experience in daily life. If you become overwhelmed by a sensation (or thought or emotion), you can bring to mind your Inner Resource, and you'll be surprised how quickly you return to a relaxed state of mind. I especially recommend using this at night when it's common during the menopause to wake up feeling anxious and overheated.

In this exercise, you create a place in your mind or a situation that gives you the feeling of safeness and calmness. The act of working and the sense of it is the critical thing. Remember, feelings may follow later. Your Inner Resource is unique to you. These examples are only suggestions, and yours might be different from these.

It could be a special place, one you've been to or a place you would like to go. It can be a place in nature like a beautiful wood where the leaves of the trees dance in the breeze. Or, your place may be a beautiful beach with a crystal blue sea stretching out to the horizon where it meets the ice blue sky. Your safe place can be being with a special loved one, a childhood home or a room where your favorite things surround you.

These are examples of possible pleasant places that might bring a sense of pleasure to you. The important things are to focus on a place that gives you feelings of calmness, ease, security, safety, and happiness. Create you Inner Resource with as much detail as possible

*Engage in your soothing rhythm breathing and when you're ready to try to create a place in your mind:*

- *Imagine looking around you, what can you see? It might be a beautiful wood where the leaves of the trees dance gently in the breeze. Mighty shafts of light caress the ground with brightness. Or, it may be a beautiful beach with a crystal blue sea stretching out to the horizon where it meets the ice blue sky. Or, relaxing next to a log fire.*
- *Now focus on what you can feel, like the sensation of the sun on your face or a breeze caressing your hair. Alternatively, can you feel soft, white fine sand underfoot, which is silky to the touch?*
- *Next, think about what you can hear. Can you hear the rustle of the leaves on the trees, or birds, or crackling fire or the gentle hushing of the waves on the sand?*
- *Now think about whether you can smell anything such as the salty smell of the sea or the smell of wood smoke or the sweetness of the air?*
- *When you bring your safe place to mind, allow your body to relax. Think about your facial expression; will enable it to have a soft smile of pleasure at being there.*
- *Imagine that, the place itself takes joy in you being here. Allow yourself to feel how your safe place has pleasure in you being here. Explore your feelings when you imagine this place is happy with you being there. Even if it is a fleeting sense of where the image might be, try to create an emotional connection to this place.*

Learning to focus on these experiences is helpful if blocks and barriers arise (especially those linked to ideas that you don't deserve it in some way) recognize these 'distractions' and go back to focusing on your safe place. We are trying to stimulate certain brain areas for you in these exercises. Don't worry if your 'distractions' seem overwhelming at times Smile to yourself. Go back to soothing rhythmic breathing and try to stay with the exercise as best you can.

## In Summary

- The beautiful thing about practicing kindness is you don't have to look far to know if you on the right track. Are you meeting your daily experiences with kindness? When you feel discomfort or are trying to resist something you don't like or want to happen can you soften into the background? To forgive yourself and move on, developing positive relationships with your changing body. Be kind to yourself. Care for yourself and your body with great tenderness and, if you slip up, don't beat yourself up!

- Our body is an intelligent system that communicates with us. It whispers at us when something is out of balance. When we ignore these signals, it turns up the volume. If we continue to ignore it, it resorts to screaming, bashing us around the head to try and grab attention. During the menopause, this seems amplified. By practicing mindfulness and developing deepening compassionate awareness and acceptance of our body, we can manage the hormonal and mood swings with greater equanimity.

- Practicing grounding, and developing a robust Inner Resource, when you feel your body is running the show, will immediately bring into the present moment. That will bring about a sense of calm and control to the situation. It is that simple.

- Cultivating a habit of doing a Body Scan daily will help you become more aware of your body. And help you to awaken our innate capacity for hearing even the subtlest of cues. This helps you to become better able to find balance and calm. You are more able to stimulate the soothing and contentment systems of the brain.

# CHAPTER 3

# GETTING CLEAR AND CALM

*All our feelings, thoughts and sensation are the like the weather that passes through, without affecting the nature of the sky itself.*

*The clouds, winds, snow, and rainbows come and go, but the sky is always simply itself, as it were, a 'container' for these passing phenomena. We practice letting our minds be that sky and letting all mental and physical phenomena arise and vanish like the changing weather. In this way, our minds can remain balanced and centered.*

*Without getting swept away in the drama of every passing storm*

*\* Segal, Williams & Teasdale[1]*

## Chapter 3.1 Brain Fog is Real!

That moment of not being able to think straight or forgetting critical information at critical junctions. What if it happens at an alarming frequency? I have had women tell me they could forget the names of close friends, their children or even their partners or get them mixed up. Or, they forget what they were doing and burn the dinner. All of these, of course, create some stress and tension. But, it is at work is where 'brain freeze' can cause the most issues.

Many women reported that these moments were amongst the worst part of the menopause because of the knock-on effects. They were often left feeling incompetent and losing confidence in themselves. That's a feeling I can relate to. It used to happen a lot to me. I'd prepare for a meeting, I knew my stuff, I was confident, well after 20+ years' experience, I should be. Then I'd get to the meeting, and the words didn't come out of my mouth, my brain couldn't process anything. It was a "brain freeze." I'd leave the meeting feeling incompetent. And then I made the situation worse by allowing my thoughts to create stories that added to the under enormous strain that I already felt. The majority of women are going through the menopause without any support at work. Moreover, the worst part of feeling mentally 'dumb' is becoming more stressed, which leads to feelings of overwhelm. That can result in adrenal fatigue, which this can lead to even more significant problems, like inflammation, rapid aging, and other illnesses.

Menopause is one of the most significant changes we women will face. "Brain fog," or "brain freezes," which includes forgetfulness, difficulty concentrating, and thinking is one of the most commonly experienced symptoms. The lapses many women have are real, and they can begin at the onset of perimenopause. It's like mild cognitive impairment, but it's not a sign of permanent degeneration. The good news is that most women who experience menopause-induced memory loss report that their memory returned after the menopause. I can say that my 'brain fog' where my mind does a complete blank in a meeting or when talking with loved ones has become a rare occurrence. And if it does happen, my mindfulness practice supports me to manage the situation. The thought patterns that lie under the surface itching for an opportunity to kick off feel under control.

Both short-term memory and recent memory are affected during perimenopause and menopause. Being able to recall names, dates, and addresses can evade a woman experiencing memory lapses, primarily if it is recently acquired information. No wonder so many women think they've got Alzheimer's or another cognitive disorder. Although much of the reporting has been subjective to date. But a new study conducted at Brigham and Women's Hospital, Massachusetts General Hospital and Harvard Medical School[2] in Boston has provided objective evidence of 'brain fog. The study found that a woman's performance on specific memory tasks tends to dip as her estrogen levels drop. This happens during the average age range of menopause: 45 to 55.

But, is 'brain fog' purely down to a drop in female hormones? The evidence suggests a mix of hormonal and lifestyle issues

## Brain fog, hormones, and lifestyle

Ovarian hormones have a direct impact on the brain, especially the areas of the brain that control verbal memory and function. The hippocampus and prefrontal cortex that is rich with estrogen receptors. Estrogen increases levels of essential brain chemicals like serotonin, which is linked to positive mood. Falling estrogen levels might be why we are snappy and irritated at the slightest thing. Moreover, estrogen is essential for the production of acetylcholine, a chemical that is essential for learning and memory. Estrogen also promotes the growth of new brain cells, the formation of synapses, and acts as an antioxidant to protect the brain from free radical damage.

It's also possible that estrogen indirectly causes memory loss by contributing to lack of sleep, mood swings, and stress. Higher levels of the stress hormone cortisol during menopause can increase anxiety and depression and may contribute to mental decline. Before menopause, women stay mentally sharp longer than men, but during menopause, women's rate of mental acuity declines. This is in part due to drop-in testosterone, which women also need it in lesser amounts.

The poor sleep that many women experience during menopause due to night sweats disturb their regular sleep patterns, and often women wake up feeling far from rested. Sleep is vital for the consolidation of memory, so tiredness can affect the way you think.

Although decreases in hormones, elevated stress and lack of sleep are likely the most common causes of memory loss in menopause, lifestyle factors can worsen the effects of 'brain fog.' These risk factors include:

- Alcohol, especially drinking above the 14 units a week advocated as the healthy limit for women. Though moderate amounts of red wine about five units a week can help keep memory loss at bay. This is due to resveratrol which protects brain cells from free radicals.

- Some medications (sleeping pills, antidepressants, pain-killers, blood pressure and heart medications)
- Vitamin deficiencies especially Vitamin D. Try to spend time outdoors every day without sunscreen (5 or 10 minutes is enough) And if you don't get enough sunshine vitamin year-round look at dietary options or supplements.
- Poor diet especially one that is low in omega-3-fatty acids like the ones found in fish and certain vegetables. Look at ways you can incorporate more these into your diet
- Dehydration is common among women in menopause. Both estrogen and progesterone are essential for fluid regulation, and lack of fluids can cause a decline in cognitive function
- Lack of exercise is bad for any brain, but a workout is positive for both your body and brain. Exercise helps the growth of nerve cells and blood vessels in the brain. Also, it increases the production of chemicals that promote the repair of existing brain cells.
- Belly Fat is linked to cognitive decline. Research shows that middle-aged women who are overweight can improve their memory and impact brain activity by losing weight

A fun and the helpful way if brain fog makes life difficult for you is to remember simple stuff like phone numbers or passwords, break them down into segments. Focus on remembering one section at a time to make recall easier. A smart way to remember new names is to associate the name with an image. Like your body, your brain needs regular exercise to stay strong and healthy. Treating your brain to mind games such as crosswords, puzzles, and sudokus are an excellent way to strengthen your memory. Moreover, it has been shown that as little as one hour a week of 'brain training' can decrease your risk of cognitive decline.

I'm especially fond of the Yoga for the Brain[3] books from coach Cristina Smith. These games include inspiring quotes and soothing pictures to bring mindfulness into the heart of puzzling. Learning a second language, dancing, or learning a new skill, such as woodworking or knitting might also be good at keeping the fog at bay.

While brain fog may not be an illness, many women want relief from it, and they have turned to HRT. If hormones are the likely culprit of menopause brain fog, it seems logical that hormone replacement therapy (HRT) would be the answer but research has repeatedly shown that HRT does little to protect against mental decline, dementia or Alzheimer's disease. However, there has been some evidence that women who used testosterone gel experienced significant improvement in learning and memory. This form of treatment may become a way forward in the future.

The key thing to remember is that brain fog is very real and that you're not going mad, nor will it be permanent. There is evidence both scientific and anecdotal that memory "bounces back" after menopause.

## Chapter 3.2 Coping and Calming the Anxious Menopause Mind

Frequent, troubling high anxiety, or panic attacks, are not a regular part of menopause and if you suffer from these, you should consult your doctor. But, many women experience mild anxiety through the menopausal change. This is due to fluctuations in estrogen and progesterone. Estrogen changes have a direct effect on the neurochemical's serotonin, norepinephrine, dopamine, and melatonin, that play an integral role in emotion and mood regulation. It's not surprising that a decline in estrogen levels can lead to mood disturbances. That, in turn, can create feelings of anxiety during the menopause.

Stress is linked to the onset and aggravation of anxiety as it alters hormone levels. Stress causes a rush of cortisol, adrenaline, and other chemicals into the bloodstream that prepares the body for fight or flight. This response triggers the physiological changes associated with anxiety, such as rapid heartbeat, slowing digestion, diverting blood flow to major muscle groups. Cortisol and adrenaline interfere with the production of the calming, soothing neurotransmitter serotonin. It becomes a bit a double whammy in the menopause when your body is producing less of the soothing neurotransmitters.

Moreover, then when you are stressed your body produces stress hormones that further depress serotonin. Finding a way to reduce stress is a step in the direction. And that is the role that mindfulness plays. It helps you to become less of at the mercy of your hormonal changes.

## How Mindfulness Helps

Mindfulness is a proven stress reduction tool that balances hormones that go awry during menopause. It can decrease the stress hormone cortisol, and this helps you to move from an aroused, stressed state to a more reflective, calmer state.

As you may have learned from the last chapter mindfulness is more about experiencing rather than thinking. The human nervous system is hard-wired to evaluate experiences and to assess them as unpleasant, pleasant or neutral. This labeling when we're stressed or anxious tends to make us overuse our minds, in mindfulness we call this the 'doing' mode. Moreover, if we spend all our time here, it can keep us trapped in our stress and anxiety. Take for example the embarrassment of your mind going blank in a key moment. You start thinking "Oh no not again, why is this happening now. Everyone thinks I'm useless". So, the first dart of embarrassment gets added to as you chastise, blame and criticize yourself.

Mindfulness lets us experience the world as it is and to let go of over-thinking. Focusing on sensory experiences is called the 'being' mode. It's not that we're trying to live like this all the time. Thinking, planning, problem-solving and the like are important but if we're feeling anxious or stressed we couldn't think our way out of the situation. Instead, the 'being' mode gives us a break and a time to be in the present moment. This is why many mindfulness practices are breathing exercises, where we focus on direct physical experiences.

## Breathing

Your breath is like the tide of your life, and for centuries people have used breath to let go of stress. How many times haven't you been told to 'take a deep breath? ' When you feel stressed or anxious your body tightens. The energy flows to muscles, and your body tries to get as much oxygen as possible, and you breathe more rapidly. Your abdomen tightens, and your upper chest works harder to get more air into the upper parts of your body. For many of us, we get stuck breathing this way even when the immediate stress has passed. This shallowing breathing then signals to the brain that you are in a state of anxiety. And stress hormones continue to be pumped into your system[4].

Breathing in and out of your nose, not anything special or deep breathing, but the bare bones of being aware of breath moving and moving out the body can bring you back to the present moment. Into 'being mode.' Start with try staying with one full breath in and one full breath out. Abandon all ideas of getting somewhere or something happening and notice the quiet that comes with this type of breathing. Moreover, if your mind wanders, which it will, then reconnect with your breath and follow the physical sensations. If you do this with patience and gentle curiosity it will bring calm and kindness to you in moments when stress and anxiety feel like they are taking hold and running the show. You are reminding your mind that you are the CEO of your life, not your thoughts. Oh, and remember to give yourself credit for this short breathing practice. You're doing much better than you give yourself credit for.

One of the other ways that can help us to move from doing to being is to slow down the breathing and take fuller deeper breaths. The longer we inhale, the greater the vitality we have. Our heart rates remain low, and we stimulate the parasympathetic nervous system which is calming. When we breathe slowly it lets our brain know we are safe, and that keeps cortisol levels low. The great benefit that comes whenever we slow down the breathing is that we are hacking into a state of flow. In this state, you are activating the vagus nerve, which creates a blend of calming serotonin, feel-good dopamine, endorphins that are nature's painkillers. Plus, anandamide the 'bliss molecule and norepinephrine that help to cut down on mental distractions. What is fantastic is that flow is always available to us. You can do this walking, sitting or as an aid to falling asleep when night sweats wake you up. Women with high vagal tone are better at digesting their food, and they have stronger immune systems. And they are better at controlling negative feelings and have more positive emotions in general. All this is precisely what so many of us need during the time of the menopause and can obtain through breath.

## One Thing At A Time

My other favorite aspect of slowing down is to learn to do one thing at a time. As women, we are often multi-tasking, juggling and running to keep up with our to-do lists trying to be there for everyone. It's not unusual to be texting a friend, switching between many windows on your computer, listening to television, and talking to your child or partner all at once! Moreover, some women I know even boast about great they are at multi-tasking. Brain science is showing us this might not be the case.

Not that being quick and busy is all bad. But it tends to activate the stress-response that makes us more irritated and reactive. Something we want to avoid as menopausal women. You can help yourself by limiting the number of things you juggle at any given time to two tasks. Or work as Professor Nass[5] at Stanford University calls the "20-minute rule." Instead of switching back and forth from one task to another. Try to devote your attention to one task for a 20-minutes before turning to the next job.

I also advise learning to do a few ordinary tasks that bit slower every day. Here are a few tasks you could try to slow down:

*Walking to a meeting or from the car park to your office? Leave enough time, so you don't have to rush. Moreover, then stroll, feel your feet on the ground, notice things around you.*

*Sip and savor a warm drink of your choice. Take some time to feel the warmth of the cup in your hand, smell the aroma, taste it, feel the warmth as you swallow. Enjoy the whole experience. Notice any urge you feel to speed up and get on with things. It takes some time and effort until you become comfortable in slowing things down.*

In doing these kinds of simple mindful exercises along with breathing exercises, you can create ways of checking in with yourself when dealing with a stressful or distressing moment. As you become more attuned, you will be able to switch to the 'being' mode. This will allow you to intervene and break your stress reactions.

## Chapter 3.3 Hello Thought, Goodbye Thought

How do you care for yourself when your thoughts are racing, and your mind is preoccupied with a million things? Trying to stop your thoughts is like holding back waves on the shore. Instead of pushing away your thoughts you can learn to notice them and let them go. In mindfulness, we call this learning to look *at* your thoughts, not *from them.* Many of your thoughts are just thoughts, a stream of mental events that may or may not be true. By observing and letting go, you're not buying into everything you think, and this in itself is calming.

The straightforward way to break your stream of thoughts is to direct your cognitive resources to immediate sensory experiences. What this means is that it helps in those anxious moments to reconnect with your body and the physical world. Plant both of your feet on the ground. Take slow, deep breaths as you tune into your breathing, to the sensations in your body, and the earth beneath your feet. When you do this, you are again activating the parasympathetic nervous system. It's the relaxation half of your autonomic nervous system. This can down-regulate the sympathetic half (the part involved in fight or flight) and calm your racing thoughts.

Many easy techniques can help slow down your racing thoughts. Two breathing exercises are ones I use a lot to help women who come to me saying their minds are full and they're having difficulty relaxing or meditating will help you let go of thoughts and rest in the present moment.

*Cross your arms over your chest, with hands pointing toward your neck. Not your arms, and with your longest fingers touching each collarbone. Breathe slowly, with eyes closed or partially closed and looking at the tip of your nose. Flap one hand like a butterfly wing against your chest, then the other. Keep going, alternating hands rhythmically for 2-3 minutes. Your hands may naturally go faster or slower at some points but keep going and don't try to control your thoughts.*

It also helps if you can get space from stressful thoughts. It is likely to be especially helpful for those with worries about the future. Or those self-critical thoughts that can arise as you go through the menopause. Focusing your attention on the breath brings us into the present moment and allows your thoughts to be there.

*Start by settling into a comfortable position and gently close your eyes*

*Begin by taking some long slow deep breaths.*

*Breathe in through your nose and out through your nose or mouth. Allow your breath to find its*

*own natural rhythm. Bring your full attention to noticing each in-breath as it enters your nostrils, travels down to your lungs and causes your belly to expand. And notice each out-breath as your belly contracts and air moves up through the lungs back up through the nostrils or mouth.*

*Notice that the inhale differs from the exhale. You may experience the air as cool as it enters your nostrils and warm as you breathe out.*

*As you turn more deeply inward, let go of the sounds around you. If you are distracted by sounds in the room, notice them and then bring your attention back to your breath.*

*Try not to change anything about your breath. Or try to control your breathing in any way. Observe and accept your experience without judgment, paying attention to each inhale and exhale.*

*If your mind wanders notice your mind is wandering.*

*Then bring your attention back to your breath. Your breath is an anchor you can return to again and again when you become distracted by thoughts.*

*Notice when your mind has wandered. Observe the types of thoughts that hook or distract you.*

*Noticing is the richest part of learning. With this knowledge, you can strengthen your ability to let go of thoughts and focus your awareness on the qualities of your breath.*

*Watch the gentle rise of your stomach on the in-breath and the relaxing on the out-breath. Allow yourself to be completely with your breath as it flows in and out.*

*You might become distracted by pain or discomfort in the body. Or you may notice feelings arising, perhaps sadness or happiness, frustration or contentment.*

*Acknowledge whatever comes up including thoughts or stories about your experience. Simply notice where your mind went without judging, pushing it away, holding on or wishing it were different.*

*As this practice comes to an end, slowly allow your attention to expand to take in your body and then your surroundings. When you're ready, open your eyes and come back.*

*And know that the breath is always with you as a refocusing tool to bring you into the present moment.*

It's good to reflect after the practices and ask yourself a few questions:

- Did you notice your thoughts and were you able to let them go?
- Did you get caught up in some thoughts and then come back to the breath?
- Were some thoughts that you couldn't let go of or that kept returning?

Experiment with these two mindfulness practices. Notice how by holding our thoughts more lightly we can let go of unnecessary thoughts and let our minds naturally quieten down. It does require practice if you're new to mindfulness. You might notice your mind has wandered off. But with time you'll get more skilled at seeing your thoughts and letting them come and go.

## Coping with Difficult Thoughts

We have somewhere between 30 - 70,000 thoughts a day, 98% of them are thoughts we've had before and 70 - 80% are negative. That's a lot of stuff swirling around in our heads, and of course, much of it connects to your emotions and the way you perceive the world.

Sometimes it is hard to let go of your thoughts; they can be compelling and persistent. Sometimes they are essential thoughts, and we need to take note of them and act on them. At other time our thoughts can feel "real" even when they're not, especially if they are emotionally charged. Amongst the women, I spoke with some had difficult thoughts that became mountains in their minds. They felt lost in anxiety and isolated, which was frightening. Anxiety can create a vicious cycle, the more you think, the more you feel anxious, and the worry makes you worry (and on and on). Part of the struggle was no one expected anxiety to be part of the decline in estrogen.

Many women spoke of their thoughts being irrational like "I have a headache, maybe I have a brain tumor!" or "My boss didn't say hello they're going to sack me for incompetence!" where anxiety had taken hold and created a narrative that wasn't founded on more than a thought. The menopause is challenging enough without having to always worry about every symptom you're experiencing. So, what can you do about it?

You can be with the difficult thoughts which sounds counterintuitive. Moreover, there a couple of options you can try when thoughts feel charged with emotion. At first, you may not notice the benefits of mindfulness, feeling calmer and more at ease especially if your anxiety or tension is intense. But, if you pay attention, then you might notice a small oasis of calm. This will grow as you practice it grows and becomes larger than your suffering. It doesn't mean you anxiety, or painful thoughts have gone away they are being held inside a bigger container. You're experiencing your difficult thoughts in a calmer way. The Three Minute Breathing Space is an excellent way to bring a calm moment into your day. It can be done anywhere and at any time.

*Breathe. Use the breath to interrupt your anxious thoughts. Bring awareness to your breath and the process of breathing in and out, the actual movement of the body as you breathe. Notice your thoughts and let them go if you can. If not try to take your attention to the emotion and see if you can feel it in your body. Can you allow and let go of any resistance to it on the out breath? Do this for a few minutes and then let stop.*

*Interrupt Your Thoughts. If you are not overwhelmed by anxiety, then you can try to interrupt the rumination. Ask yourself questions like "What am I feeling right now?" This gives you another option to meet your anxious thoughts rather than getting tangled up in an argument with them.*

*Labeling the thoughts rather than accepting them as facts, or reality can be helpful. For example, I am having thoughts that I am unlovable. In this way you separate fact from fiction, taking control back of your thoughts rather than being consumed by them*

Reflecting on your experience is important. When do you get anxious? What raises your anxiety? One of the most important ways to treat your anxiety, especially if it escalates, is to understand what your triggers. The more you understand what makes you uncomfortable, the better you can tackle the root of your anxiety. If this becomes a regular occurrence, then seeking help from a professional trained in approaches like Mindfulness Cognitive Therapy (MBCT) can support you to cope.

## Chapter 3.4 Acceptance versus Change: The Paradox of Mindfulness

You are probably reading this book because you want things around your menopause experience to change. If you are anything like I was, you might be looking to feel calmer, less overwhelmed by the hot flashes and the brain fog and the negative mindset that all this creates. And therein lies the paradox of mindfulness and the theory underpins it that can be hard for people to get their heads around. I know, because I've had to work through this as I developed my mindfulness practice.

It's all connected to acceptance. Mindfulness meditation involves being open to what is happening in the present-moment experience. Allowing whatever is happening to be there without your natural tendency to want to distance yourself from it or change the experience. To let the unpleasant experiences to be there rather than pushing them away or trying to cling to pleasant ones. Moreover, all the while ignoring neutral ones.

Mindfulness sharpens your ability to witness thoughts as they arise by not hating negative experiences or distorting the appreciation of a pleasant one by grasping after them. Witnessing is a neutral stance wherein we place no judgment on our thoughts. Instead, we observe what passes in front of us as a neutral witness, and this allows us to see the larger picture that so often escapes us. There are real benefits to mindfulness, which begin with and are maintained by, letting go of the need to improve or change our menopause experience at a given moment and becoming a witness to our menopause experiences instead.

Mindfulness and meditation are not always the Zen-like experience depicted on social media. The interplay of your body and mind with each other and the world can be downright messy. If you sit down to practice mindfulness with the goal of being less stressed, you may become disappointed. And you might even feel more stressed and anxious. Moreover, you can have added the feeling of irritation or failure. And most likely you will have reinforced the notion that, beyond being unpleasant. You may start feeling stressed is unacceptable and that it must be eliminated from your life. The next time you feel anxious or stressed, and you try to make it go away with mindfulness, you'll feel trapped in a situation you've convinced yourself is incompatible with ease. And that's more than unpleasant, that's suffering. This is often why I have heard clients who've previously tried mindfulness say, 'it doesn't work.'

Mindfulness meditation is best practiced without striving for an outcome. Learning to observe your experience, with an attitude of curiosity. Are we supposed to accept everything and do nothing? This paradox is real. As we become more established at witnessing we realize that all thoughts are transitory, they are continually changing. Developing the capacity to welcome and be with all our thoughts without repressing or reactively expressing what we feel or think creates as if by magic a shift. By our willingness to meet, greet and welcome our thoughts we go beyond them. The word experience' means to go through something entirely, leaving no trace behind.

It's possible to accept the difficult experiences and also work to change the unpleasant aspects of the menopause. In truth, the awareness and wisdom that comes from a regular mindfulness practice will help you be more effective in managing the stress and anxiety that arises for many of us during the menopause years. In mindfulness, when we speak about letting go we're talking about the goal to change, avoid, or cling to your present-moment experience. This is different from encouraging the wholehearted acceptance of all your menopause. It's more about saying "at this moment, this is what it's like" than "it is what it is, get used to it!" Acceptance never means stoically putting up with or resigning to stressful situations. Acceptance is not a passive negative one but one that is positive, active and that gives us a willingness to engage with our experiences.

Some things we can't change and mindfulness has supported countless other women to accept the intractable aspects. Our bodies are changing. Our minds can, at least in the short term, be a bit compromised. And we will have difficult days when the symptoms want to overwhelm us. This might seem a bit fatalistic to say we have to accept. But if we let go of the resistance, the unhelpful untrue thoughts, the harsh negative thoughts and judgments we suffer less which in turn means we feel less controlled by these events even if they are still a part of our experience.

People who practice mindfulness meditation try to bring present-moment awareness and acceptance to their daily lives while working on a long-term goal of changing things. I practice mindfulness to reduce suffering whenever possible. And reduce the amount of new suffering that I cause to myself and others through my thoughts and actions. This helps me to keep on the path to becoming a happy, compassionate, and true to myself as possible. Moreover, in my book, it is okay to practice mindfulness with those kinds of goals.

Practicing mindfulness daily so that you aren't only doing it when things feel complicated, and you're seeking instant relief. Then you will find you break the association with short-term gains and begin to see the benefits of coming closer to with your life experience, which is more significant than immediate gratification. There is no quick fix where mindfulness concerned. The benefits that emerge from having mindfulness practice are many, including a greater sense of calm and well-being. As well as becoming less emotionally reactive, having lower stress levels, greater empathy, and an improved quality of communication with others.

## In Summary

- Clear, calm mind allows you to be your healthiest, happiest self. Sure, it's easy to dismiss brain fog and anxiety as a function of late nights, busy schedules, and substantial to-do lists. But, you owe it to yourself to stop making excuses. Remember, just because your life and menopause symptoms are deemed "normal" doesn't mean you can't take control and ease them. A little mindfulness goes a long way toward helping you calm your thoughts, feel more clear-headed, confident and content.
- Your breath is your friend and is always with you, and you can at any time make a choice to deal with thoughts that are stressful or anxious by focusing on the breath and interrupt a cycle of thinking which can 'rev up' your distress. Learning to breathe more slowly and deeply stimulate the whole body and profoundly affects your sense of wellbeing. By improving vagal tone, you can become a healthier, happier version of yourself
- Look ways that you can bring slow moments into your daily life. Like daily activities, you bring mindful attention to. For example, walking, eating, your morning coffee break, whatever fits into your schedule. Remember to observe the minds tendency to rush and bring yourself back to a slower pace.
- You don't have to believe everything you think. Thoughts are often that thoughts, a stream of mental events and you can choose to engage with them or to let them go. The Breathing Anchor meditation helps you to focus your attention back to the present moment using the natural flow of the breath.

- Remember your mindfulness practice is not a trick to get rid of your anxiety and challenging thoughts. Mindfulness is teaching you to see the bigger picture skilfully. So that your experience at any given moment is more than your thoughts or your stress and moreover, that you are not your thoughts. You're learning to give yourself a little breathing space in that stressful moment, throughout the menopause journey and into the rest of your life.

# CHAPTER 4

# THE WISDOM OF OUR EMOTIONS

*Walking the Coast*
*Knowing now*
*That the life*
*At which I am*
*Is a circumference*
*Continually expanding*
*Through sympathy and understanding*
*Rather than an exclusive state*
*Of pure feeling*
*The whole I'm out for*
*Is center plus circumference*
*And now the struggle at the center is over*
*The circumference*
*Beckons from everywhere*

*Kenneth White[1]*

## Chapter 4.1 Hormones & Our Emotions

Even writing this made me feel emotional as I went back to a time when my hormones didn't feel in harmony. You know that feeling when your emotions are all over the place. The emotional symptoms of the menopause are well documented, yet many women are unprepared for the emotional highs and lows and how their moods are influenced by hormonal changes. Especially when estrogen starts to go up and down like a yo-yo, it can get a spike and then drop steeply. and that's the point where your emotions are affected, and then there can be an outburst of some kind. Many women find that they will cry about things that they never used to worry about before. Or they cry for no apparent reason.

I remember finding myself in the car sobbing my heart out. I could not stop, and I felt this profound sense of sadness. It was almost like the world was going to end, and I felt powerless to do anything about it. I remember thinking when I had stopped crying "What on earth went down here?" Because it appears there was no logical trigger for this behavior. There was no reason for it, but you know, it feels overwhelming when it happens.

Women I've spoken to have reported they stopped watching the news because they feel emotional about every sad story. Other women find that they get more upset by other what other people are saying. They take things they would have brushed off in earlier years; now they take them to heart. Or, very often, they got the wrong end of the stick about what people are saying and became tearful.

While these feelings can be challenging, they are part of the rollercoaster nature of the menopause experience. Moreover, it has been reported in a recent US study that a quarter of women have said they are experiencing mood swings through the menopause. Amongst the women I spoke to there was a strong feeling that more women are suffering. I know of women that did not want to share these emotions at work or even with their family for fear of being seen as a hysterical or incompetent woman. This is a label that remains from Victorian times when women were locked in mental hospitals because of mood swings and depression.

As we know during the transition, there are changing hormone levels. Estrogen levels fluctuate and then decline, and your body also produces less progesterone. Both of these hormones influence the production of a neurotransmitter called serotonin. It's serotonin that regulates your mood and makes you feel like your emotions are out of control.

## How does estrogen act on the brain?

It is a complex mechanism that I've tried to explain in a few steps:

- Estrogen increases the levels of the neurotransmitter serotonin and endorphins. Serotonin and endorphin are 'feel-good hormones' that help to reduce irritability and anxiety.
- Estrogen increases the number of serotonin receptors in the brain and therefore makes the brain more sensitive to serotonin.
- It also indirectly increases the levels of other neuro-transmitters like norepinephrine that act as brain stimulants.

Researchers have also found higher levels of a brain protein known as monoamine oxidase A (MAO-A), which is linked to depression, in women entering perimenopause. Moreover, there is evidence that altered levels of female hormones, i.e., FSH (Follicle Stimulating Hormone) and LH (Luteinizing Hormone may have a positive correlation to irritation. In other words, many factors are coming together in a perfect storm that explains a large part of the emotional highs and lows during this transition.

Mood swings are amongst the first signs that you are going into the menopause transition. Women in the early peri-menopause are more prone to irritability than pre and post-menopausal women. But, due to the commonality of symptoms, many women confuse perimenopause with PMS and vice versa. Both PMS and perimenopause are the result of fluctuating progesterone levels. However, PMS symptoms are cyclical and correlate with a woman's menstrual cycle. They also disappear once a woman gets her period. Not so with perimenopause. Perimenopausal symptoms continue throughout the monthly cycle and are also much more unpredictable and intense. So many women feel as if they are losing control or going crazy

Your situation and your lifestyle can be contributory factors in determining your emotional state during the menopause. Conditions and life events that tend to crowd into women's lives when in their late forties and fifties can include:

- Children leaving home
- Divorce
- Retirement (of self or partner)
- Widowhood
- Illness or death of parents
- Physical aging

Other psychological challenges can include beliefs about no longer being useful or distorted body image. Fear of death, insomnia, feeling 'unemployable,' low self -worth, and the physical symptoms of the menopause itself can impact our emotional wellbeing.

Women may be at a higher risk of emotional problems if they have complicated relationships with a partner or other close family members. Or they are coping with elevated levels of work-related stress or have other health conditions or difficult financial situations. Moreover, if your menopause is causing symptoms such as sleeplessness and hot flushes, you can feel uncomfortable, and fatigue and this, in turn, can amplify the existing emotional and hormonal changes.

There are some women for whom this hormonal flux can be severe. Then it's not a case of crying or worrying or fearing, but they can find that they become depressed. They can feel a sort of bleakness of their life, or they may find that they don't want to carry on. If this is you or someone who's going through the menopause that is feeling like this, it's imperative to get checked out by a doctor, because this type of hormonal change needs medical support.

## Chapter 4.2 You Are Not Going Crazy!

The critical thing to take away from this is, this is not all in your head. You are not going mad! It is not all in your mind. There is a genuine physical, hormonal reason for these moods. Although you think that you are falling off the cliff-edge and that there is something wrong with your mental state, that just isn't true it is just your changing hormone levels.

You need to talk to your friends and family about what's going on. There's nothing worse than a loved one seeing their Mom or partner bursting into tears, slamming doors or shutting themselves in the bathroom for half an hour. It is important that they understand that there is a real reason for this behavior. Moreover, this is usually only part and parcel of the menopause, and you'll get through it. Post-menopause your hormones do start to re-balance themselves, and you should find that the emotional episodes decline.

### What are the emotional symptoms of the menopause?

Everyone's emotional triggers are different. And it's not always easy to pinpoint what sets off your mood swings and irritability. But, many women do experience these common symptoms:

*Aggressive*

*Anger or even rage*

*Sadness, tears or uncontrollable crying*

*Lack of motivation, an apathy*

*Irritability and a tendency to bite people's heads off*

*Tension, anxiety, and nervousness*

*Extreme moods, mood swings, or quick and unpredictable changes in mood*

*Feeling way more sensitive to things that never fazed you before*

*Feeling reclusive and not wanting to join in or be sociable*

*Less patience for your children, or changes in your willingness to accommodate others in your family, you may even resent your children*

*A lack of enthusiasm for sex or uncontrollable sexual urges*

Does this describe you? You're not alone. However, it is a powerful emotional ride. These are some of the most common emotional symptoms that clients, friends, and colleagues have shared with me and that mirror my own experience of the emotional side of the menopause.

## Irritability

There are some days where everything gets under your skin. In the past, if you were standing in the supermarket queue and somebody was slow at packing his or her groceries, you would have stood there patiently being sympathetic. Whereas now, you start to get irritable and you wish they would get a move on up because you are busy. You have lots on your to-do list that you need to get done. If you find that you're getting very irritable with your loved ones, they get very puzzled by what's going on. Also, if you have teenagers going through puberty well, then it is a heady hormonal cocktail. And it can often explode and create disharmony that lasts for hours.

And if you begin to lose your patience, or you get irritable with your colleagues, you can then start to feel bad. It that can change the whole dynamics of your workplace relationship. And that, in turn, put more pressure on you until it becomes a vicious stress cycle.

In the broad scheme of things, these minor irritations shouldn't cause too much of a fuss. But when you're going through the menopause, something that generally wouldn't bother you can turn into a drama. When I was going through the menopause, the smallest thing would get under my skin. And I would feel like my day had been derailed. And the sad part was I would take it out on other people, usually my family which made me feel worse and created even more tension.

We live in a stressful world where impatience and irritability are typical behaviors. But, during the menopause, it is as if we have turned a spotlight on these behaviors. In my case, I became angry very easily. One moment I would be fine, and then something minor would set me off. I was snappy, irritable and not very pleasant to be around.

I remember getting in from work and finding my teenage son had not stacked his cup and plates into the dishwasher. It shouldn't have been an enormous issue; a firm reminder wouldn't have sufficed. But I barged into his room, screaming at him at the top of my voice. I could see a reflection of myself in the hall mirror and there I was this person going nuts! I would feel hot, bothered, my heart was racing. I am ashamed to say that these sorts of outbursts were not a one-off, trivial things he did could trigger an emotional outburst. I cannot recall how many times my son asked me "Mum, why are you always so angry?". That hit me because I'm not an angry person. The scariest part was that I couldn't explain what was happening to me. Or why I was flying off the handle at the smallest thing.

## Anger

One of the more challenging aspects of the hormonal changes during menopause that was shared with me was how it was difficult to "control" anger. A Nuffield Health survey[2] in the UK of more than 3,000 menopausal women found that 60 percent has experienced hormonal changes that made them behave differently. Or these changes had a detrimental effect on their life, with uncharacteristic, irrational anger a common symptom.

Anger is an emotion that we suppress a lot in our culture. And I heard women confess of how they felt trapped and helpless in the cycle of rage and regret. The menopausal woman's mantra might often be summed by the phrase "I snapped, I shouted, I apologized."

Many women are snappy during this time which is an understandable response if you have been wide awake half the night, soaked in sweat and filled with anxiety, while your partner is sound asleep next to you, oblivious. However, what many women talked about was a frothing fury, a burning rage.

*Angie's story "My anger and rage were out of control. I've gone off sex, and my husband could not deal with that. He said we had to plan it and do it on a Saturday, so we did not lose the connection. I dreaded Saturdays. I was not interested in sex; my libido was at an all-time low*

*This caused arguments, and my rage would come out. I hated the weight I had gained but did not have any motivation (or time!) to do anything about it. The pressure also affected my sex drive. It felt like I was trapped in a vicious circle. I offloaded all my anger onto my husband. I was cruel and would say some nasty things, which then left me feeling depressed and guilty afterward. I was sabotaging my marriage and felt like I might lose my husband. He was driving me crazy. But, exercise, along with meditation, helped me to slow down and channel my emotions. It was not easy, but it certainly saved my marriage.*

## Fear

Then there is fear, and this a significant emotion that can emerge. You can start to feel fearful about your future even about the future of the world. You are afraid of what's going to happen to your family. These thoughts are sometimes irritational. And can include thoughts that something dreadful is going to happen.

The feeling of fear can also be that you are entering a new life. Moreover, many women say to me, "I don't know what's going on. I can't plan for anything. I don't know what's going to happen. "There's also the fear of your changing body image as this is the point when you might start to notice things changing. So, you fear that your looks may be going, you might not be attractive anymore, which is a big issue for many women.

There's also the fear of relationships. Unfortunately, when women are experiencing many mood swings, their partners do not always understand what's going on and this that can lead to arguments and disquiet. So, many women fear for the health and the state of their relationships. Because of age discrimination in the workplace, many women express concern about their ability. Or the possibility of a promotion. Or that they will be among the first to be made redundant if their jobs are insecure.

Very often you will find that these feelings of dread kick in as you're waking up in the morning. When you're asleep, the ancient part of your brain is still active. Our evolution has created us to be always a little bit aware of our environment in case of attack. It is a pure survival mechanism. So, there's still a tiny part of your brain that has a bit of awareness of what's going, when you are asleep. Unfortunately, when you first wake up, if these fears or worries kick in, then that part of the brain will go set off the fight or flight mode, and everything becomes magnified. Everything becomes a threat. Moreover, you can then get caught up in this fear and anxiety until your rational brain kicks in and then goes, "Oh, it's time to get up."

None of these emotions are your imagination talking. HRT is often prescribed for mood swings. There are suggestions that tiny amounts of estrogen may be beneficial in improving mood But the evidence of the effectiveness of HRT in treating psychological symptoms is inconclusive. So, it is also important to look at the contributing factors that you can control. Lifestyle choices and finding mindful ways to work through painful emotions can play a significant role in how you respond to these mood shifts.

## Chapter 4.3 Learning to Work with Your Emotions

Your emotions during the menopause can be difficult and to prevent being swept along by them; You need to cultivate a resilience to be able to tolerate the feelings the menopause throws up. Through exploring and staying open to our emotions, you can learn to regulate your feelings and attend to them even if they are unpleasant.

How can you open up to your mind states and be curious about them? How do you stay open to exploring the exact flavor of the emotion? Mindfulness teaches us that emotions like thoughts are not facts. But signals arising from the brain and body based on our experience and situation. Instead of trying to change the emotional experience with cognitive approaches or trying to get 'rid' of the experience, you take time to soothe and regulate it by accepting, knowing and allowing. One way to skillfully relate to experience is to register the moment and hold it in awareness as a body sensation.

## Riding the Waves

When you apply mindfulness to emotions, you discover that emotions are like waves coming and going. Waves cannot be fought but need to be allowed to break over and then flow away. It is the same with emotions. There is only learning to make peace in this moment., rather than trying to control how you feel. Becoming mindful of your feelings at the moment as a cluster of body sensations and responding by accepting and embracing what you are feeling. If you do this, you may notice that you become less fearful, less ashamed of and less attached to your feelings.

## Dealing with Feelings

Directly feeling your emotions may be painful but makes room for responding to them with kindness and creativity. When you can reflect on them, then you can find your considered action and cultivate a sense of wisdom. The Buddhist monk and Nobel Prize Laureate Thich Nhat Hahn[3] has outlined five steps way of dealing with strong emotions.

- *Recognition: Be specific about the emotion you are experiencing. You could say "I know there is irritability in me" You can label the specific sensations that* go with *this emotion "I am feeling hot, flushed, tense.."*

- *Acceptance: When you feel an intense emotion, do not deny it. You can accept it, be present and think "I accept that I am experiencing intense irritability right now."*
- *Embracing: Hold your emotion in your arms like a mother holding a child. Let your mindfulness embrace this feeling. This step can soothe and calm you. It is an act of compassion, empathy, and responsiveness to your distress. Moreover, is much more effective than rejecting or punishing yourself for this emotion.*
- *Reflecting: When you feel calm, you can reflect and try to understand the triggers to this irritability. Even though moods can feel out of control during the menopause, there are still triggers that can cause your discomfort. You may find that have a particular value, belief, expectation or judgments that kick in and create an emotional response. These may have been with you, but pre-menopause you had stronger control over them.*
- *Insight: Bringing understanding of the conditions that trigger your emotions can help you know what to do. How you can change situations and how to look after yourself.*

## Anger - The Most Difficult of Emotions

*"You should be angry. Use that anger. You write it. You paint it. You dance it.*

*You march it. You vote for it. You do everything about it. You talk about it. Never stop talking about it."*

*— Maya Angelou[4]*

The absence of serotonin itself does not necessarily make you angry, but it may make it harder for you to underplay your feelings. There are times when we are fully entitled to express that anger, effectively, proportionately, and to the right recipient. Yes, you're probably going to blow up but cut yourself a little slack. Be as open as possible with loved ones about what you're going through to limit the collateral damage. Moreover, be ready to apologize, and forgive yourself.

Better still channel that energy because it is a big, powerful emotion. You can use that energy to drive change. So take deep breaths as many as you need, open your mouth, and speak your truth.

Nurture yourself when you're feeling rage in constructive ways. Meditation, visualization, and practicing gratitude can be effective. Invent a dance, grab your journal and start writing, cook up some great food. You feel full of energy and will feel even better when that energy is released. Especially if you have something positive to show for it rather than another apology. And remember you are entitled to your emotions, hormone-heightened or not. Suppression, guilt, and avoidance of your emotions is not a positive way to live through the menopause or at any other time of your life.

## Chapter 4.4 Mindful Ways to Cope on Difficult Days

Emotions get stronger if you fight them. But if you can learn to anchor difficult feelings, you can avoid getting caught up in mental anguish. There are some ways that you can use the sensory anchors of the breath, the body and nature to develop a softer, friendlier relationship with painful emotions.

### Welcoming the Opposite

Research on emotional resilience shows that to navigate life, you need to be able to name the emotion you're experiencing. And describe the feelings that make up your experience. Mindfulness meditation can help, by teaching you how to observe, identify, and respond instead of reacting. Every emotion comes paired with an opposite. Anxiety cannot exist without peace. Fear cannot live without courage.

Moreover, helplessness cannot exist without its opposite, empowerment. When you experience only one-half of a pair of opposites, you are stuck in a one-sided view of life. But, if you can open to the full range of emotions, you can break free. Of course, suffering from something like severe anxiety is not so easy, but there is an exercise that I learned that could provide relief.

This meditation focuses on welcoming the emotions you are feeling and then concentrating on the opposite of those emotions like embracing a feeling of peace when you're angry. When you welcome your difficult emotions, it helps you to shift from being stuck in negative or destructive reactions to recognizing more positive and constructive responses. When you're open to welcoming and experiencing every emotion, as well as its opposite, negative emotions no longer control your life. Self-judgments do not take hold and are replaced by kindness and compassion. Simultaneously welcoming opposing emotions deactivates your brain's default network and limbic system, which hold you hostage to negative emotions. It activates your brain's defocusing network, which enables you to gain insight and perspective, which in turn make you less reactive and more responsive.

*Begin by connecting with your surrounding with your eyes open or closed*

*Feel the air on your skin, the texture of the surface you are resting on, any sounds inside and outside the room*

*Welcome an emotion that's currently present at this moment or recall an emotion that you have recently experienced. It does not have to be a negative one. Notice where and you feel this emotion in your body without judging or trying to change it. Welcome your experience just as it is.*

*Next, think of the opposite of this emotion, noting again where and how you experience this opposite in your body. If helpful, recall a memory that invites this opposite more fully into your body.*

*When it feels right, let yourself move back and forth between these opposites, sensing how each emotion impacts your body and mind. When you're ready, sense both emotions at the same time, again noting these feels in your body and mind.*

*Now, move between experiencing a feeling of well-being and your two chosen emotions. First, experience well-being then each emotion and then experience both emotions plus well-being at the same time. Note how your body and mind feel as you do this.*

*When you're ready, take a deep breath and affirm that as you go about your daily life, sensations of calm and well-being will be with you in every moment. When you're ready, open your eyes and return to wakefulness, thanking yourself for taking this time. It is good to journal your reflections and intentions that emerged during the practice. And to agree with yourself to follow through with these as you go about your daily life.*

Here are some examples of emotions and their opposites. But do not feel you have to limit yourself to this list. Find emotions that are relevant and meaningful to you and your experience.

Aggressive - Passive

Peaceful - Angry

Calm - Agitated

Safe - Threatened

Confident - Insecure

Trusting - Suspicious

Delighted - Disgusted

Unafraid - Anxious

Generous - Resentful

Unreserved - Shy

Happy - Sad

Vital - Exhausted

## Breath as an Emotional Regulator

As the body reacts to a highly emotionally charged stimuli, stress hormones take over sending the body into survival mode. The emotional brain is susceptible and reacts to anything that is perceived to be a threat, whether it is indeed a threat or not.

As you have guessed by now that I am a big advocate of deep breathing as a way to anchor yourself back to the present. Belly breathing, in particular, helps you gain emotional regulation skills by helping you to access executive functioning, something was done intentionally. One of the best ways to do this is to learn to take fewer deeper breaths. Some people advise taking 12 breaths a minute to get optimal blood flow and circulation to the rational brain and help create a pause between an upsetting event and the reaction. Ed Harrold, one of the world's leading mindful breathing experts, recommends slowing the breath down to 4 deep breaths a minute, in and out of the nose. I have done this many time when my emotions have spun out of control, and it works!

Furthermore, counting breaths taps into the brain's emotional control regions. And controlling breathing by counting breaths influences "neuronal oscillations throughout the brain," Particularly in brain regions related to emotion. Studies had shown that brain activity in areas linked to emotion, memory, and awareness showed a more organized pattern when controlled breathing was carried out. Perfect for settling the 'out of balance' menopause moments that countless other women and I experience.

## Mindful Movement

How we move and stimulate our bodies subtly but potently influences our emotional state. It has long been understood that exercise neurochemically acts on and within the brain. While studies have focused on benefits to cognition and mood, the crux here may be what happens at the moment rather than what comes afterward or builds over time. As a mindfulness teacher, I encourage and use movement with my clients to help them deal with painful emotions. Through movement, they can come into a flow state, which becomes a re-grounding in sensation. Flow provides physical and emotional reassurance that we are OK. The action itself can become the antidote to overwhelm.

Walking or running mindfully are great ways to practice moving without a goal. Mindful moving like this means walking or running while being aware of each step along with being aware of your breath. It can be practiced anywhere, even between business meeting. You can move at your pace if you want you can keep your steps slow, there is no need to rush, no place to get to, no hurry. Mindful walking and running can bring peace to your body and mind.

To make the mindful movement more useful for dealing with challenging emotions that you may have I particularly like the approach developed by psychotherapist William Pullen called Dynamic Running Therapy (DRT). In his book *Running With Mindfulness*[5], he explains that at the heart of this therapy is self-acceptance ". It offers a way to learn to be more accepting of who you are inside and of the things that have already happened to you. It helps you value what is real in the here and now, not the stories that you tell yourself."

Pullen's DRT to include these three stages in the walking or running

1. **Ground**. Become present, step away from the busyness of the day and to prepare yourself for DRT.
2. Begin by doing a quick *Body Scan*. Sitting comfortably, settle into your breath and use your awareness to scan through different areas of your body, feeling and breathing into any areas of tension with gentle, soothing breath.
3. *Environment Scan*. Shift to take into your surroundings, noting your sensory experience, the smells, sounds, tastes, and sights.
4. *Emotion Scan*. Become aware of any emotions you are holding in your body at this moment. Be sure to focus on what you are currently feeling not past emotions

5. *Priming.* Choose a question to focus on. For example, you may ask yourself, "Where does the majority of my anxiety come from?"

6. **Intention**. Once you begin moving; walking or running "Hold on to the question of the day gently. Allow it to wash around you." Notice when your mind wanders, which it will, and be patient and gentle with yourself. It's not about doing it correctly.

7. **Reflect.** Keep a journal of your experience. As you record your progress, notice your emotions and how you relate to yourself through the process. Part of taking notes is recognizing that whatever your pace, you are moving through this experience and change is happening.

## Connecting with Nature

We all need to do more getting outdoors and connecting with nature! Because of how we live there is a massive disconnect with nature. Science is showing us spending 2 hours in nature can reduce our stress by up to 800%. So that seems like a pretty significant reason to spend time more time outside.

As a Scandinavian, I know that the forest is a place to unplug, feel calmer and even to awaken my spiritual side. Forest bathing or *shinrin-yoku* is a Japanese practice of going out into the forest to improve health and for wellbeing. It was promoted in 1982 by the Japanese government[6] to encourage people to immerse themselves in nature. Trees have healing properties that enhance our moods. Forest bathing has been found to relieve stress, by activating the parasympathetic nervous system.

The way to practice forest bathing is to stop and using all our senses become attuned to forest life:

- The colors of the foliage
- The sounds of the forest
- The texture of the bark, and feel of the ground underfoot
- The smell of the flowers and the undergrowth

Try to get out into nature at least once or preferably twice a week, completely unplug and let nature do its healing work.

## In Summary

- As you enter perimenopause, the estrogen levels in your body begin to go up and down and then decline there can be an emotional response. Mood swings are amongst the first signs that you are going into the menopause transition. Irritability, anxiety, fear and even rage can emerge. Though hormone imbalance may look a little different for every woman, it can catch you off guard but remember that it's another stage of your life. With awareness, support from your menopause expert and a few simple steps, you can navigate it with grace.
- Although HRT helps to balance the hormonal levels in the body, your emotions during the menopause can be painful. It is helpful to cultivate resilience to be able to tolerate the feelings the menopause throws up. Mindfulness teaches us the emotions like thoughts are not facts. But signals arising from the brain and body based on our experience and situation. Instead of trying to change the emotional experience with cognitive approaches alone or trying to get 'rid' of the experience. You take time to soothe and regulate it by accepting, knowing and allowing.
- When days are difficult then movement, breathing, spending time in nature and meditating can all help to calm these emotions. They help to anchor you in the present moment. Slowing down your breathing to four breaths a minute, connecting with the full sensory experience of a walk-in nature or practicing working with opposite emotions help to activate the parasympathetic nervous system. They assist the body in producing much needed 'soothing hormone' and help you to learn to 'surf the waves.'

- As you become more familiar with being able to witness and work with your emotions, you will see that they are continually changing. You can learn to develop the capacity to welcome and be with all your emotions rather than being a slave to them.

# CHAPTER 5

# REWIRING THE NEGATIVE THINKING

*I have come home*
*From self-imposed long exile*
*To this imperfect body*
*Comfortable in my discomfort*
*Welcomes, like the Prodigal Son, returning*
*No blame*
*No Guilt*
*No recrimination*
*Only love*
*So simple*
*Loneliness healed*
*Now everyone is welcome*
*To my home*

*Gary Hennessey[1]*

## Chapter 5.1 Yes, I Should, I Should, I Gotta

I should, oh yes, I have to!

How often don't we let our lives be ruled by "shoulds", the fear and procrastination? I know that was a lot of the time. The menopause doesn't give us an option. We can't procrastinate about whether we want it to happen or put it off indefinitely. So, for many women, it feels like they ended up in a situation where they have a low locus of control. Moreover, this can bring our self-sabotaging behavior to the forefront and make the menopause feel more like a struggle. But, the menopause also affords us the opportunity to change the way we view ourselves and our place in the world.

Your "shoulds" are shaped by neural programs that often operate unconsciously or semi-consciously or sometimes hiding in the shadows. Plus, in a deep sense, your "shoulds" can control you. (unlike healthy principles and desires, which you're able to reflect on and influence.) We move towards what feels good and away from what doesn't. These behaviors can then become internal rules - "shoulds," "musts," and that's the big problem. We can end up feeling driven, righteous, or failure. At their root "shoulds" are about what you want to experience (especially emotions and sensations) and if your demands on reality are met, or what you fear you'll encounter if they're not.

During my menopause, it felt like I'd doubled up on my self-sabotage ability and in turn, it made me more stressed, which in turn in created more stress and unhappiness - a never-ending circle. As I've explored further what I've found is that this self-sabotaging behavior can ground in:

**Fear of change**: Our brains are wired to be on the alert for danger. It's part of our survival mechanism, so we can prepare ourselves to survive the outcome best. So, we like to stay consistent, and we find it difficult to embrace change. If our happiness depends on achieving our goals as envisioned. Or through events unfolding according to our wishes. Or our bodies meeting certain societal 'norms' then we are condemning ourselves too much misery. In psychology, this is called, "cognitive dissonance." When actions, events or our bodies don't line up with our ingrained beliefs or values. Then we feel uncomfortable. Moreover, try we try to rely on the safety of the status quo and therein lies the problem.

**Low self-worth/Low self-esteem**: We grow up with stories about negative self-worth that don't serve us. Unfortunately, they become imprinted into our brains, and they get replayed over and over. Often, they go like this: You don't deserve to be happy. Why do you think you should be able to have it all? Do you think you deserve to go on holiday? Other people are beavering away, and you want to take time out?

I'm pretty sure that you could make your list from your self-talk. We feel that we aren't good enough, that we lack in some way. Over time our sense of inadequacy continues to grow, casting doubt on even our smallest dreams. These doubts and insecurities get reinforced today on social media, TV shows, and movies. Here the standards of what is said to be required to be beautiful, to be a good parent, a good partner as prerequisites for happiness, success, and love get reinforced.

**Need for control**: It's not surprising that peri-menopausal and menopausal women feel a loss of a sense of control given the hormonal swings and roundabouts going on. If we can control our outcomes rather than letting someone/something blindside us, we feel less uncomfortable. Research has shown that way in which we appraise our menopausal symptoms and the strategies we use to cope along with our perception on how much we believe we can control our symptoms affects our sense of wellbeing. It was seen that women who had lower levels of an internal locus of control suffered more than women who practiced proactive health-conscious behavior. Women who adopted healthier lifestyles around diet and exercise, yoga and mindfulness report fewer symptoms even those women who turned to their doctor for HRT which is an example of an external locus of control.

**Procrastination**. Why not put it off for a day or two? It won't matter. These are words of a self-saboteur and one of the most common ways we shoot ourselves in the foot. We can't stop the menopause from happening, but we invent what we believe to be legitimate excuses to delay taking better care of ourselves. Ultimately, by delaying or not practicing self-care, we are further fuelling the flames of self-sabotage, stress, ill-health, and unhappiness.

**Addictive behavior:** Often we develop blocking behavior to helps us to manage which can include self-medicating with alcohol, food, or "retail therapy"? How about binging on an 8-hour marathon of Netflix. I can remember telling myself, "It's a great show, I'll watch one episode" Or having a glass of wine that rather than taking time to meditate or go to the gym?

Dropping the "shoulds" can make you feel you vulnerable, and that can be hard. We use "shoulds" to try to hold back the pain and loss we can face during the menopause. The loss of our youth, our fertility, our old self and of course some women feel this more than others. The pain and loss that we experience will happen regardless of our "musts" and "cant's." It means we're deluding ourselves by thinking that this issue of rules will somehow hold back the menopause tide.

## Chapter 5.2 Becoming Aware of Our Inner Critic

Let's face it; there is no-one who can beat you up as much as yourself. I was an expert at this. We all have some level of self-talk going on, and unfortunately, that talk often takes on a negative tone. I have had to work on this, i.e., not beating myself up. Through my mindfulness journey, I came to realize that allowing negative talk free rein dragged me down and cut me off from moments of joy and created further stress. That, in turn, reduced my confidence and self-esteem and were the worst kind of messages I could send myself.

But, who is judging who? Our inner critic, that voice that stresses us out more than any other person. It was once described to be not as a small voice but a gorilla in a dustbin that wants to get out and wreak havoc in our lives. That made me smile but also touched a nerve. When feelings of stress, anxiety or even panic arise, it can feel like we've put on glasses that distort reality and make it more worrisome.

Sleepless nights, sweating into the sheets. Our weight yo-yoing means we're not happy with our bodies. When we have 'brain fog' at important times or snap at our loved ones without knowing why the internal dialogue becomes "What's wrong with me?" "I'm worthless," "Why can't I be fabulous?" These messages assume something is "wrong."

These inner habits of the mind lead to more automatic thinking. We spend more time monitoring our thoughts and feelings in ways that lead to even more unproductive rumination. It's not working through things although on the surface it looks like it. It can lead instead to more self-criticisms. More comparing, more rigid rules, more judgment, more self-attack and more isolation. As an activity of the mind, allowing your inner critic free rein takes up an enormous amount of real estate in our consciousness.

Mindfulness and acceptance can interrupt the spiral of distress. By giving attention to the experience, rather than ruminating on it. Moreover, it can be helpful to become familiar with the style of negative thinking that is your default. Find out which is your preferred unhelpful thinking pattern. Becoming aware of this. So, when it occurs, you can catch yourself doing it earlier and choose a different response.

## Habitual Thinking Styles

*Catastrophizing* - *this my preferred style of negative thinking where we amplify anxiety, expect disaster. And then play out in your head the worst outcomes. A game of 'What If?*

*Discounting the Positive* - *Here we follow every statement with a but. So even something good is put into a negative context. This can make us anxious and even depressed.*

*The Eternal Expert* - *This heightened stress as we always are on our guard to be right. Being wrong is not an option, and we must defend every opinion and action.*

*The Shoulds* - *This can lead to guilt when our unbreakable rules get broken by ourselves*

*Blaming* - *This involves criticizing ourselves when we make mistakes*

It might take some work, but over time you'll notice the voice that is upsetting you the most and the times at which you are most vulnerable. Late at night, before bed? When you look in the mirror on a morning when you don't feel great?

Now, have I've reached a point where at the very least, I am aware of this and If I slip (and I do) & beat myself up. I forgive myself. Remember becoming aware of our thoughts and messages, involves many levels, layers, and depths. We have thinking patterns that have built up over a long time. So, we need to practice, notice and honor what we're thinking. And then learn to reframe the dialogue to be "There Is Nothing Wrong with Me"?

There isn't anything wrong with you. You are a woman. The menopause is the most natural thing. It is part of being a woman. But, when we send a message that something is "wrong," to yourself, we create stress, anxiety, and fear. That creates more tension, worry, low mood & on & on it goes.

The good news is that science has shown that our brains can be re-wired to form new pathways, new ways of thinking. This is the process called neuroplasticity. It is said that "Nerves that fire together, wire together." And by having the same thoughts over and over our brains build specific neural pathways. By re-training our brains to think more positively, we are making new more helpful and supportive neural pathways. We can change our brains and our thinking away from our critical self to a kinder more loving self.

## Chapter 5.3 The Journey to Finding the Positive in You

Imagine what it would be like to drop your "shoulds" and the inner critic as you go through the menopause? What would this feel like? Relaxing, easing, and freeing - quite possibly. You can go through the menopause no longer chained to "shoulds" and the negative self-talk.

By opening to this tide as it runs in your life, a more profound reality than can ever be contained by your thought occurs. You reduce the uncomfortable feelings imposed by "shoulds" and increase your sense of opening into being carried by life's beautiful stream. When the "danger" is the painful emotions that rise our response can be self-criticism, self-isolation, and self-absorption. These, in turn, impact our health and happiness. Turning to the positive helps us view uncomfortable emotions as less of a threat.

So how do you do that? Start with mindfulness. Neuropsychologist Rick Hanson[2] has summarised what in three steps: let be, let go and let in. Or, as he describes it through this metaphor

*"Imagine that your mind is like a garden. You could be with it, looking at its weeds and flowers without judging or changing anything. Second, you could pull weeds by decreasing what's negative in your mind. Third, you could grow flowers by increasing the positive in your mind."*

**Let be**: We can be mindful of negative thoughts or feelings when they arise and being aware of our thoughts or feelings diminishes their power.

**Let go**: Sometimes, being with negative thoughts or feelings is enough for them to fade away. In most cases, though, it requires some conscious effort to let them go.

Two things I love about Rick's teaching is the advice that we do this when it feels right. The time for letting go of our negative thoughts or feelings varies based on what we're experiencing. It would not be healthy or comfortable to try to "let go" straight after an unpleasant experience. But, if it's a common worry, you might be able to let it go shortly after recognizing it.

Begin letting go: Often, you can't "drop" the negative thoughts or feeling but, you can begin.

**Let in**: When it feels right. That after you've released some or all of the negative, you replace it with something positive. It feels better to dwell on the positive versus the negative. Moreover, the benefit goes much more in-depth. The brain learns based on your experiences. As you spend more time with positive experiences, you grow circuits in your brain. In practical terms

"If you practice relaxation, this will calm down stress reactions, making you more resilient."

In contrast, "If you are focusing on self-criticism, grumbling about hurts and stress, then your brain will be shaped into greater reactivity. You will be more vulnerable to anxiety and depressed moods. You will have a narrow focus on threats and losses, and inclinations toward anger, sadness, and guilt." It's such a logical approach. Notice the negative, let it go and replace it with something positive.

Building on Rick Hanson's approach here are some proven ways to manage the natural tendency to self-sabotage. And how you can bring more of the positive into your life to support you through this time of your life

## Let Be: Exploring Your Thoughts

Most of us have harsh inner critics who judge us, put us down, and punish us when we don't live up to some internal or imposed ideal. I've always found it amusing that the inner critic is so often described as a small voice. I much prefer the metaphor that it is a gorilla in a dustbin that gives half the chance would like to come out and wreak havoc on my life if it could. That has always encouraged me to act. And if you can see your inner critic more in this light (feel free to have your mental image of it) then rather than beating yourself up for having negative self-talk, you can take affirmative action.

The first step to action is to begin to explore these negative thoughts and 'shoulds' in some detail. You can start by recalling one of your menopause-related situations (I'm sure there are many) and see if you can find a central "should" in your reactions to it. It might be saying to yourself things like "that can't happen," or "this must happen," or "I can't t stand ___," Notice how they should always are framed as if they are real. While in fact, you should is a thought or many thoughts. Thoughts are a stream of mental events.

*Then, try asking yourself "Is this should true? "Sit with the answer. You might find that the "should" is not true at all.*

By facing our reality, we can begin to see how these thoughts, once they get free reign, can develop a life of their own. How they drag you out of reality and cut you off from moments of joy. This simple moment of recognizing the truth pulls you out of the stories and into direct experiencing, which can help you gain clarity, calm and a sense of freedom.

You can go continue to deeper into these situations and what you will find as you ask yourself again "Is it true?". Often it is never as bad as our imagination of what could happen. You can take some further time to explore your thoughts, to notice and honor what you are thinking. Often when we're busy, our thoughts are fragmented, incoherent and don't make sense. Images, half-finished sentences, disconnected phrases, and dream-like states happen to all of us and from my personal experience were very prevalent during perimenopause and menopause. Sitting quietly, we can listen and look at patterns in our thinking. Always do this with gentleness, permission, and curiosity.

*Sit and notice if there are ongoing stories that have a coherent theme and a flow to them. Explore these by asking yourself a few questions. Note down what you observe.*

- *Who is the voice that's speaking?*
- *How does it speak to you? Can you describe the tone, the perspective, and quality of this voice?*
- *Is it kind, harsh, irritated, forceful, nagging?*
- *Who is the audience? Is it you or others?*
- *What is the theme and flow of the story? Are you trying to be understood, convincing, defending, criticizing?*
- *The ask again 'Is it true.'*

We are much more resilient and capable than we think we. Please don't think I'm trying to minimize or dismiss how awful the menopause can be. Or that self-critical, judgemental thoughts that arise can sometimes feel challenging, painful and overwhelming. But, by recognizing that a "should", a negative thought, isn't true can help you to 'loosen 'up these painful and unhelpful thoughts. It can help you to make space between the thought and the fact so that they can be differentiated. Good news is you're on the way to putting the gorilla back in the dustbin and learning to sit on the lid.

## Let Go: Building the Foundations for Self-Love

"When we can see ourselves as we and accept ourselves, we build the necessary foundation for self-love."

Sometimes accepting and letting go of that former self can feel like killing part of who you once were. And this because our identity as a woman is formed through incredible resilience and strength. So, it can be hard to let go of that woman without also feeling like you're letting go of the subtle strength that got you there. It can feel as if you are grieving and your loss gets reflected in our negative self-talk around the menopause.

But, we can let go of our negative thoughts and their associations. I have found that meditative practices that support me to let go of negative thoughts about the changes my body was going through have been the most helpful. The ones that help me to come to terms with the fears of what I would become and the losses I was experiencing. One of my favorites is a standard technique used in Acceptance and Commitment therapy called 'Leaves on a Stream''. The essence of the practice is to gently and consciously place your thoughts on a leaf and watch them float away. Cognitive distancing[3] is a process where under certain circumstances we choose a different relationship with the stream of thought that flows through our heads. This changed relationship can be characterized by:

- more distance from negative thoughts
- more mindful, i.e., observing our thoughts rather than swept up with them
- less willing to take our thoughts seriously, i.e., thoughts don't often correspond to the breadth and depth of reality

- more focus on direct experiences, e.g., feelings, observations, sensations

*Sit comfortably in a quiet space. Relax your body, take a few deep breaths and prepare to spend the next 10 minutes letting go of thoughts.*

*Visualize yourself sitting beside a this gently flowing stream with leaves floating along the surface of the water.*

*For the next few minutes, take each thought that enters your mind and places it on a lambda; let it float by. Do this with each thought - pleasurable, painful, or neutral. Even if you have happy thoughts, place them on a leaf and let them float by.*

*If your thoughts stop, continue to watch the stream. Sooner or later, your thoughts will start up again.*

*Allow the stream to flow at its own pace. Don't try to speed it up and rush your thoughts along. You're not trying to hurry the leaves along or "get rid" of your thoughts. You are allowing them to come and go at their own pace.*

*If your mind says, "This is dumb," "I'm bored," or "I'm not doing this right" place those thoughts on leaves, too, and let them pass.*

*If a leaf gets stuck, allow it to hang around until it's ready to float by. If the thought comes up again, watch it float by another time.*

*If a problematic or painful feeling arises, acknowledge it. Say to yourself, "I notice myself having a feeling of boredom/impatience/frustration." Place those thoughts on leaves and allow them to float along.*

*From time to time, your thoughts may hook you and distract you from being present in this exercise. This is normal. As soon as you realize that you have become side-tracked, bring your attention back to the visualization exercise.*

*When you're ready, you can open your eyes and return to the room.*

I'm a huge fan of writing down my feelings, my thoughts and my judgments. During the menopause It allowed my soul to express what it was feeling in a safe space. Moreover, it created a piece that I could come back to and reflect on when negative thoughts started to take hold. You can write this on a piece of paper, but I prefer to use a book.

Here's one way that I have used and continue to use. I like to call it A Menopause Prayer

*Find a quiet space for at least 5 minutes.*

*Sit down with a pen and paper or a notebook*

*Take a few deep breaths, ground your feet on the floor*

*The ask 'What do I need to let go of today.'*

*Write, with the flow and without judgment*

*It's OK to cry, your giving soul space*

*When the flow of words stops, then you put down your pen*

## Let In: Take back control and H.E.A.L

Learning to let go of the negatively charged thoughts that arise during this transition time. Of wondering who you are, of feeling overwhelmed by all the changes going on, takes some effort. But, once you're on that journey, you are creating space for positivity. The best way to bring to let in the good is to learn to turn to the positive. And let it have more space in your thoughts, in your life.

Find activities that encourage stillness and positivity like yoga, qi gong, or writing in your journal. Ask yourself what you used to love doing when you were younger? Or, reflect on things you've longed to do but put off doing because of work or family? Don't make it too big or too complicated. But instead look for small things you could do on a regular basis that can be placed into your life, replacing time spent in front of the TV or scrolling social media. Any right brain activity, like singing, dancing, art, knitting, and pottery, helps you to find positivity in small, simple things, like spending time with friends or family that uplift and support is a powerful tonic.

Inner strengths we need to help through the menopause such as happiness and resilience come from embedding positive experiences into our brains. To do this, we need to do a bit more than enjoy the experience we need to pay mindful, sustained attention to them. Otherwise most positive experiences flow through our brains like water through a sieve. We notice the momentary pleasure they bring. But they leave little lasting value on changing our brain, of changing in effect its neural structure. As psychologist Dr. Rick Hanson says "The brain is like Velcro for negative experiences but Teflon for positive ones".

To make these small positive steps even more powerful and help the brain to build new pathways we can practice a technique developed by Rick Hanson called H.E.A.L. This stands for Have, Enrich Absorb and Link. The HEAL practice helps rewire our brains to have more positive thoughts. In detail this is how the practice works:

**HAVE** The first step is Have, and you can either have a positive experience right now good food, a great cup of coffee being with friends, watching a movie, seeing a sunset or playing with your kids. If you can't do anything these things, then try at least to recall a recent positive experience. The important thing here is to recognize that the experience doesn't have to be "special" it can be an ordinary experience you have every single day.

**ENRICH** Because of the Teflon nature of our minds we usually have positive experiences, and they come and go without us paying much attention to them. The "E" stands in H.E.A.L stand to Enhance or Enrich because for us to create more positive neural pathways. We need to practice having these positive thoughts for longer than a few seconds. Try and see if you can stick with the positive experience for at least 5 seconds, longer is of course better. Now, enhance it by imaging what it feels like in your body. What feelings come with the experience? What else can you notice that is pleasant? Stick with your positive thought with a broad, open body, mind and spirit. Continuing along this vein of extending the experience we move to:

**ABSORB** This is a "taking-it-in" practice. Hanson points out that while we remember the good stuff, we don't always take the time to let it sink in. How many times haven't you sip a coffee or eating a biscuit while working or watching TV and never noticed how great they tasted. Absorb involves the mental process of allowing the positive experience to sink into your body, mind, and spirit. To help me I visualize my positive experiences being like the light that seeps into every cell of my body. As you recall that positive event, enhance it, let the memory sink into you, into your heart, into your body, taking it in. Consciously absorb the positive qualities.

Doing these three steps several times a day for no more than a minute is enough to begin the process of seeing your world in a more positive light.

**LINK** The last step "L" is for Link, and this requires more skill than I can write about here in the book and so this a brief introduction to the Link part and I suggest that you read Dr. Hanson's book called Hardwiring Happiness. Recall a negative experience that you might want to "rewire." We have plenty of those during the menopause, but I recommend picking one that's not too distressing. Recalling what I love about my body then recalling something I've said to myself that was difficult. I bring the positive, enhanced, absorbed memory to the fore while keeping that challenging moment in the back of my mind. I let the two mix together. Hanson says, "what goes together grows together." I do this several times, so the next time I find myself saying something mean to my body, I've created a positive memory association link. Could you give it a try? I think you'll be quite surprised at the results.

H.E.AL Have, Enhance, Absorb and Link is the practice that takes in the good and links these experiences with more negative, challenging thought patterns and rewires our brains to the positivity we need during the menopause. By drawing on the hidden power of everyday positive experiences, this deceptively simple practice builds resilience, heals distress, promotes physical health, and makes us feeler happier.

## Chapter 5.4 Celebrate the Change

As we begin to let go of our negative thinking patterns, it becomes vital that you become mindful of your vocabulary. Stopping the chimp chatter that perpetuates this time as anything but ordinary, and very powerful. Many women go through the menopause blaming forgetting something on a "menopausal moment." Or who talk about their sexuality by saying "I am all dried up." These types of statements support the continued messaging of disease and disorder. A more empowering way of speaking could be "I have been more forgetful lately, I need to see what might be contributing to that."

Approaching the menopause with positive thoughts lets us see it is a massive shift. But one that can provide opportunities to heal and grow. The menopause is a shift, a transition and metamorphosis into a new phase of your life no longer oriented towards reproduction and caring for the family. But instead, a time when going deeper into your own life. A time where intuition and creativity can grow. Respect the menopause and the growth that comes with it with gentleness and curiosity.

The more, as we start on the journey to re-wire our brains to more positive thoughts about the menopause, the more we can see the changes that we're going through as a way to harness our feminine power and celebrate. In our society, we see it as natural to celebrate marriage and childbirth as essential transitions in a woman's life. Moreover, some women even celebrate divorce. Why don't we celebrate the menopause? Or say WE CAN. We can change societies view of the menopause when we decide to drop the negative language and choose to celebrate all the positive things, little by little, day by day. Women live over half their lives after menopause. It is not the end of anything. It is the beginning of one of the most powerful and enlightening times and can be filled with a sense of renewal and hope.

Here are my three top reasons to celebrate the menopause:

- *Your children are growing up and becoming adults who can take care of themselves. You can drop the role of housekeeper, cook, chauffeur to name but a few. This frees up more time for you and the things you love to do. It allows you to make meals that you enjoy and eat at times that best suit you. You can have your home back the way you like it.*
- *If you've suffered from PMS and painful periods, the menopause frees your body from the roller coaster ride of the menstrual cycle. Get back those days each month you spent suffering from cramps and bloating. Moreover, you're freed from the fear of unwanted pregnancies. Plus, you can take the money that used to be spent on tampons, pain relievers, and birth control and spend it on something you want.*
- *You can rediscover your youthful dreams, hopes, and desires or create new ones. Look how many women in their 50's become entrepreneurs and start doing things they love and have had to put off because of family commitments. Or, take up a new sport, a hobby, go on a trip of a lifetime. We can say yes to our dreams, to what you'd like to do, not what others would want you to do. The menopause gives us an opportunity to keep learning. To take up studying or get new skills and in return, the brain will respond to positive neural changes that will serve you as age.*

## In Summary

- All of us have some form of negative self-talk and should go on in our heads. And the narrative they create can lead to more self-criticism, comparing, self-attack and condemnation. During the menopause, it is natural to want to move away from unpleasant mental and physical discomfort. But it far from helpful.

- By starting to observe what our thinking and habitual patterns of thought are like around the menopause, we can learn to watch them like clouds in the sky. We can begin to recognize that they sometimes they aren't true but a stream of mental events. By creating distance through mindfulness and acceptance practices, we can learn to interrupt this spiral of suffering.
- Gentle practice like "Leaves on a Stream" supports us to let go of our rumination, our shoulds. And metaphorically we can see them floating away down the stream and creating space for more positive thinking. Letting go can become the rule and not the exception in the way we approach the menopause.
- Use H.E.A.L as a foundational way to build more positive neural pathways in the brain, you are developing a more positive, kinder approach to the menopause symptoms, opening the possibility to see this phase life as a transformation to a newer wise you.
- There is a clear case that making time for positive reflection can help many women emerge positive, refreshed and revitalized. Even happy and proud to have 'managed' their menopause and look forward to the future. It is time to celebrate the menopause as we do marriage or having a baby in ways that are supportive of our wellbeing.

# CHAPTER 6

# BECOMING YOUR OWN BEST FRIEND

*Your grief for what you've lost lifts a mirror up to where you're bravely working.*
*Expecting the worst, you look, and instead here's the joyful face you've wanted to see.*
*Your hand opens and closes and opens and closes.*
*If it were always a fist or still stretched open, you would be paralyzed.*
*Your deepest presence is in every small contracting and expanding, the two as beautifully balanced and coordinated as bird wings.*

*Rumi[1]*

## Chapter 6.1 What Is Compassion?

Compassion has been the hardest and the most valuable part of my mindfulness journey to date. I have learned to rewire my response to the menopause and to life itself. For a long time, I wore a mask, well more like a thousand disguises. Masks that I was afraid to take off and none of them were me. I wanted to give the impression that all was OK. Underneath as the menopause kicked in was confusion and in honesty fear. I became obsessed with my appearance. I cut my hair short, bought endless new clothes, waxed, plucked, and dyed. I considered plastic surgery and exercised every day. I was determined to keep my body younger, slimmer, more attractive. I would never allow myself to age. I even lied on dating sites and in person about how old I was.

Moreover, my body reacted to this. I had gastric problems, and my blood pressure kept rising. My body and I were at war for quite a few years. As my mindfulness training got underway, everything went well until the compassion part. I got stuck, and couldn't connect with' practices, which was evident to my teachers and mentors. I recall Karen, my mentor, asking me if I'd run off time when I worked through this part of my training. The answer was an honest NO! The solution was to make peace with my body, mind, and soul the way I looked and felt. I had to accept my changing body for what it was to restore my health and emotional balance.

I began to stand in front of the mirror and to reconnect with every part of my body, forgiving myself for every flaw and imperfection. After a while, I could look at myself and accept what I saw. Free from judgment. From this point onwards, it became easier to care for my body, my whole self; my health improved together. But, acceptance isn't compassion. The breakthrough for me was developing the skills of compassion.

Developing compassion can be a way of bringing our emotions into balance in a way that increases our sense of well-being. Compassion helps us to recognize that we have self-worth. It teaches us that it is worthwhile for us to become more sensitive to our feelings and thoughts. But, as we've discussed earlier, it's also about learning to respond rather than react. To be open and able to notice our feelings without being overwhelmed by them. To tolerate them and to understand and think about our feelings and thoughts. Moreover, to be able to this without judgment. Over time we become kind and mindful towards ourselves.

Of course, the opposite of compassion is emotional reactivity, isolation, self-judgment, and unhealthy perfectionism. All of which have been linked to depression, stress and reduced quality of life. The root of this is often fear. Several of the women I spoke with in researching this book stated that they needed information, not compassion. Compassion was dismissed as weak, as touchy-feely or irrational, or they were even frightened by it. It was strange to them because they had never been compassionate towards themselves. One woman felt that compassion was letting her off the hook, that it was in her world 'first world twaddle'', a soft, easy option. Those of us who have worked with compassion now that it is far from a natural choice.

Compassion doesn't try to sweep everything away or only soothe. Compassion gives us courage through the menopause to confront our change with kindness. This kindly approach helps us to face our anxieties, our physical, mental and emotional difficulties and find peace within the menopause.

Research has found that compassion may have a profound effect on us. Studies show that when we feel compassion, our heart rate slows down, and we secrete the "bonding hormone" oxytocin. The areas of our brain linked to caregiving, and feelings of pleasure light up, which often results in our wanting to care for ourselves and of course other people.

My own experience is that mindfulness and compassion practices are visceral. Moreover, that's the point. Self-compassion isn't an intellectual exercise. It's not one where we fight the self-critical thoughts in our heads with logical arguments. Instead, it's a warm, loving, connected attitude and feeling, one that exists in our bodies as well as our minds.

## Compassion and Self-Compassion

Psychologist Kristin Neff[2] doesn't distinguish between compassion and self-compassion. Self-compassion is treating ourselves as we would a best friend who was suffering. Neff describes this as involving involves three steps:

- Mindfulness: Being aware of our situation, without becoming consumed by it.
- Common humanity: Recognizing that our suffering is part of being human
- Self-kindness: Caring for ourselves by soothing our pain and offering ourselves understanding.

"What we're practicing with self-compassion is "what do I need at this moment?'. Can we give ourselves what we need?" says Neff.

In those moments of self-care, we can also make loving gestures toward ourselves. You might want to put one or both hands on your heart or hug yourself. The key is to experiment and find a gesture that brings you a sense of comfort and warmth.

But not all self-compassion feels warm and fuzzy. Neff believes that self-compassion has a yin and yang. The yin is its comforting, soothing form, where we validate our pain and acknowledge our difficulties. The yang is the more motivating form of self-compassion, where we protect.

Compassion has tremendous benefits for both physical and mental health and our well-being. What happens when you act more compassionately? Researchers have studied this topic, and the results are impressive. Compassion, as it turns out has many health benefits that can help us to navigate the physical, mental-emotional aspects of the menopause.

## Boost the Immune System

The latest research on inflammation, which is associated with cancer and other diseases high in people who live under much stress. Cole and Fredrickson (2) found that people who were happy because they lived a life of pleasure had high inflammation levels. While people who were happy because they lived a life of purpose or meaning had significantly lower levels of inflammation. Part of living through the menopause is finding and living to our mission, which I'll explore more in Chapter 8.

## The Stress Connection

A 2017 study[3] found that people who have higher levels of compassion handled stress better. The key reason cited was because they are less reactive in stressful situations. They spent less time dwelling on stressful events. The implications for health are significant. We know that chronic stress harms health and cause spikes in blood pressure and blood sugar, along with suppression of the immune system. People can develop 'blocking' behaviors to manage their stress. These can include unhealthy coping mechanisms such as smoking or numbing their feelings with food or alcohol.

The study also found that compassionate people are more likely to adopt health-promoting behaviors and maintain them. These behaviors are especially important as women go through the menopause. Healthy eating, sleep, and exercise is all behaviors that help women to navigate these years with greater ease. Moreover, compassion has a positive effect on our mental well-being. It appears that compassion takes the edge off negative emotions such as fear, frustration, and disappointment. It helps the person to care for themselves instead of getting derailed by their situation. One of the reasons that compassion protects against stress is that it is pleasurable. That sounds good.

## Chapter 6.2 Learning to Love the New You

Compassion starts with attention. Being able to attend to our physical sensations and our thoughts, as we discussed earlier. It's about being able to think and reason helpfully and to bring warmth and kindness to ourselves so that we can behave rationally and compassionately. We know as discussed in Chapter 3 that when we dwell on anxiety other negative feelings, we lock in these feelings.

But, compassionate thinking and behavior are more than being" nice "to ourselves. Sometimes it's more about being honest and at times being willing to tackle difficult thoughts, painful physical sensations, and feelings. But, this doesn't denigrate caring for ourselves. There are times when we need to recognize the importance of rest, relaxation or everyday fun.

Compassionate behavior also helps us to develop the courage to act against the anxiety that the menopause can bring. To do what we don't want to do or stop doing things that might be unhelpful. It helps us not to take the path of least resistance that might give us temporary relief. As this way can include over-medicating, but ultimately doesn't lead to anywhere. And instead to do things that are conducive to our well-being even if they feel harsh at the outset.

As mentioned if we are very self-critical becoming self-compassionate can also feel like a threat. The important thing is the intention to become more self-compassionate. Setting intentions can help us to navigate the day to day realities of the menopause. Intentions are always personal and lend support for helping us to become kinder and having a greater sense of well-being. You can set intentions for each of the stages of the menopause unfold. I recommend you set an intention for each day. Some key tips are to

- Keep the wording positive
- Be concise and active
- Phrase your plan in the present tense, as if it's already true

I like and recommend setting intentions each morning following this approach:

*In the morning, spend five minutes meditating or journaling about what you plan on doing that day and why you are doing it.*

*Contemplate "What is it I value?" and "What, in the depth of my heart, do I wish for myself?"*

*Set the intention like "I welcome and nourish feelings of well-being". Or "Today, I am mindful of my body, and I relate to myself with kindness, understanding, and less judgment."*

*Before you go to bed, consider with kindness if you met your intention. Were you able to do something that brought it to life, such as staying cool when a hot flash threatened to derail your meeting? Did you take time out to pause and relax?*

*Repeat over days and weeks; reinforcing this exercise makes compassion come more easily and feel even more fulfilling.*

Nurturing ourselves in this way can help to develop the characteristics of a compassionate person. Professor Paul Gilbert[4] describes four essential qualities that make up someone who is kind. Wisdom, strength, warmth, and responsibility. Cultivating these qualities can profoundly allow us to navigate the menopause with greater ease.

**Wisdom:** We become wise when we recognize that we are the product of our genes and our experiences. Moreover, that we can learn, change and grow. The menopause in many ways is such a profound change that if we approach it with wisdom, we can emerge as a new person, closer to our "ideal' self". Taking time during the menopause to reflect through meditation helps to recognize how complicated life is. We can drop the black/white world and step into a world of multi-colors. Compassionate wisdom gives us the opportunity to understand how unhelpful our inner critic is. And teaches us the ability to become kinder to ourselves is the key to the honestly treat ourselves like we do our loved ones and best friends.

**Strength:** This strength is an inner sense of confidence that comes from wisdom. It gives us the determination to meet the changes of the menopause with courage and fortitude. We can imagine ourselves as more significant than we are, wise women coming through our difficulties. We can do this by breathing, rhythmically and deeply.

**Warmth:** The tonality of compassion is gentle but firm, it's an open friendliness. We can stop being 'nice' which is often something women are told to be from childhood. Instead, we are intent in a warm and friendly way to be caring towards ourselves and others. Knowing our boundaries and being unwilling to cross them.

**Responsibility:** This aspect is related to our commitment to ourselves to be our best, even if it's small steps at a time. It's about continuing to reframe our inner critic, stop blaming and talking ourselves down. Instead, we act in ways that are helpful towards ourselves based on wisdom, strength, and kindness.

One way to begin becoming a compassionate self is through visualization techniques. I found this exercise helpful for my clients and me. It's simple, yet effective. Visualization harnesses one of our significant and often untapped skills, the imagination. Moreover, it's a skill that works well with mindfulness in this context as mindfulness helps us to find the balance between conscious intention and free-form thinking. Remember that even if you don't feel these qualities, see them in your mind. Regular practice will help.

*Find a warm, comfortable place, free from distraction. Sit rather than lie down as this will help you to stay with the visualization and not fall asleep.*

*Begin by setting the intention of being a compassionate woman*

*Prepare to allow yourself to go with the images that arise without analyzing or rationalizing.*

*Relax and let go of tension in your jaw, around your eyes, shoulders, neck, hands and anywhere else you feel that you are holding tension*

*Bring a gentle smile to your lips, soften your facial expression*

*Focus on your breath, feel your diaphragm moving as you breathe in and breathe out until you have a soothing rhythmic breathing*

*The recall the visualization intention*

*Let it carry you to a beautiful, safe space, and there in front, you are a path*

*You prepare to walk that path to find your compassionate self*

*In your own time, you start to walk the path which stretches up a hill*

*Waiting there at the bottom of the hill is a guide who will provide you with all you need to travel the path*

*As you climb, remember to take a rest and to believe in yourself*

*Soon you will reach the summit, a beautiful, magical place.*

*There waiting for you is a wise teacher, you recognize that this is yourself*

*Wise and having wisdom, an understanding that comes from knowing your body and your mind*

*You take this moment to see yourself as having strength, confidence, authority*

*You feel yourself standing tall, your expressions confidence, calm and sensitive*

*You continue your journey along the hilltop path*

*You feel in this magical place warmth and kindness*

*You hear someone speaking in a gentle, caring tone, and realize that this is you*

*You continue along the path with a sense of freedom in heart, a lightness in your step, where there is no blame, no criticism*

*Absorb the presence of your true self*

*When the experiences feel complete, express gratitude to your true self and begin the descent down the hill to your safe space*

*Now return to your physical body, feel your feet on the floor and your body seated on the chair*

*Slowly open your eyes and return to the present moment*

## Chapter 6.3 Recognising Your Inner Beauty

Compassion profoundly touches us, and this is because it's connecting us to our inner wisdom. During this transformative part of our lives, we want to be cared for, cared about and connected to others. A fantastic way to strengthen our sense of our wise, strong self is to practice gratitude. When we open our hearts to positivity and accept our compassionate self, we sow seeds that help us to transform. Gratitude is the ultimate form of self-care. It's tending in a gentle, loving way to our own needs first. Then we can then serve ourselves from a place of love, energy, and abundance. Gratitude makes us feel good and makes us want to share that bounty with those who could use a little uplifting.

When I completely embraced gratitude, not a conceptual level, but letting gratitude seep into my bones and cells. I was able to become grateful for everything I had rather than focusing on my circumstances and how my body was reacting to the menopause. I began to see how blessed I was. And that I didn't need to strive to try and be my younger self or one free from all the hot flashes, the sweats, and the brain fog. I could love and accept myself as I was.

Practicing gratitude during menopause is not always a natural strategy when we're feeling the effects of the menopause. Night sweats, brain fog, mood swings, weight gain and more. The word on many women's lips is "What? I'm supposed to be grateful!" Well, yes. That's not downplaying that many women have a tough time during the menopause, but gratitude helps you to manage the menopause experience better. Here's why.

## Less Stress

Gratitude affects your hormones, from oxytocin to cortisol, and your neurotransmitters, including dopamine and serotonin. Recent data suggests gratitude increases blood flow and activity in the hypothalamus, the master gland that controls hormones. Probably the most important benefits of gratitude practices during the menopause is the lowering of cortisol. That's a huge benefit. Given that our natural protection against cortisol has been reduced as progesterone levels drop in the body.

In a 2003 study on gratitude concluded that "a conscious focus on blessings may have emotional and personal benefits." Dr. Robert A. Emmons of the University of California, Davis, and Dr. Michael E. McCullough of the University of Miami recommended using gratitude exercises as a form of psychological intervention and actively starting gratitude writing on a routine basis.

Menopause can often be a time of loss and sadness for some women. But if you are thankful for something, you acknowledge that you are happy about it. Therefore, fostering gratitude means cultivating happiness. And happiness is associated with astounding benefits for our health. One of the critical factors at play here is that appreciation release the "feel-good" hormones, serotonin, furthering the connection between gratitude and happiness.

## Better Sleep

As many of us experience the menopause is a time when sleep can feel like it's fallen off the radar. Gratitude has been shown to result in better sleep and stronger cardiovascular and immune systems. One recent study equated two weeks of daily gratitude journaling with increased quality of sleep. When you sleep you release optimal amounts of the hormone melatonin, which impacts overall health and wellbeing. Given the high reported levels of poor sleep amongst menopausal women, gratitude interventions could help us to feel less exhausted and more energized.

## The Dopamine Effect

My favorite part of practicing gratitude is that gratitude begets gratitude. The more we practice, the more we want to practice because it feels so damn good. In part, this is because being grateful releases the hormone dopamine. Dopamine is the brain chemical that gives us the feeling of with reward, pleasure, and satisfaction. Once you have experienced the feel-good benefits of gratitude, you'll want to keep feeling that way. Gratitude interventions create a positive feedback loop.

## Practicing Gratitude

The fantastic thing about gratitude it doesn't have to be about the big stuff in life. It can be about thankful for the small things like sunshine, a smile or a great cup of coffee. Psychologist Robert Emmons[5], author of *Thanks! How the New Science of Gratitude Can Make You Happier*, has shown that keeping a gratitude journal and writing brief reflections on moments for which we're grateful can increase our sense of well-being.

If you're like me, you'll feel compelled knowing these benefits to rush out and buy that gratitude journal. You start writing, and then life gets in the way, and the motivation is gone. Emmons research shows that it helps to not only to start a gratitude practice but to maintain it. Here are a few ways that can help you to do that.

## Keep It Fresh

The best way to feel the benefits of gratitude is to notice new things that you can feel grateful for in your life. Gratitude journaling works because it changes the way we perceive situations. You might always be thankful for your family and friend. But writing "I'm grateful for my family" week after week doesn't help your brain to notice other grateful moments. Get specific about your gratitude moments. "Today my colleague bought me a coffee, so I didn't have to rush out to get one'. Or "My friend invited me for dinner, so I didn't have to cook after a long day. Opening your eyes to more good stuff around you can enhance your gratitude practice.

## Plan Your Gratitude Practice

It can be inspiring to feel the benefits of gratitude. Being optimistic about the benefits is also about being realistic about how difficult building any new habits is. Instead, recognize and plan for the obstacles that may get in the way of your gratitude practice. For instance, if you are getting the kids ready for school and then commute for an hour in the morning, except that it might not be the best time to focus. Instead schedule your gratitude in the evening, when you have more time.

## Make Gratitude Fun

Writing can get a bit stale and my intrinsic motivation, the sincere desire from within to persist with my gratitude can slip away. One of the most significant determinants of whether we stick with a gratitude practice is what psychologists call autonomy. The ability to do things the way we want. So, if journaling is feeling stale, try out different and creative techniques to capture gratitude. There are heaps of ideas out there on the internet. One of my favorites is keeping a gratitude jar. Any time there is a moment of gratitude, you can jot it down on a piece of paper and put it in a pot. Whenever the menopause is making you feel a bit low, you can stick your hand in the jar and pull out a grateful moment.

Incorporating gratitude into your life to help support you through the menopause journey is easy and fun. The power of gratitude can transform our menopause experience. It's the magic key that brings peace and joy into our daily lives.

## Chapter 6.4 Claiming and Celebrating Your Wisdom

I believe compassion is something we can practice that will bring immediate as well as real and lasting happiness. Moreover, the key to developing compassion in your life is to make it a daily practice. Compassion should be natural because we all want to be happy. Unfortunately, we are biologically built to avoid danger. Moreover, we can quickly go into a fight, flight or freeze mode. Show yourself kindness in ways that nurture the mind, body, and spirit. Beyond a daily gratitude practice, I also practice and recommend focused compassion practice. Remember that there are times when we don't want to practice this compassion. We can feel angry and frustrated with the changes the menopause is involuntarily placing on our mind and body. At such times we need to compassionate to our anger and frustration, it's not wrong. Instead, allow and accept the emotions and then choose how to respond.

Among my favorite practices here are some that have worked well for my clients and me. There is also a wealth of other methods that can be found and I recommend reviewing those available for free from Kristin Neff on her website http://self-compassion.org/category/exercises/

### Small Daily Compassionate Practices

Starting small is a fantastic way to begin to build a compassion habit. Here are some simple steps that can be inside your day without too many barriers. And can make a difference in the way you feel about yourself as you go through the various stages of the menopause.

- Do one small thing every day that you enjoy. It could be a walk, playing with your children or grandchildren, baking. It's your choice
- Do one random act of kindness for yourself. Ensure that is a kindness, not indulgence. So often these things don't involve buying anything but making time for yourself. You put your feet up for 10 minutes, make yourself a tea or other drink you like, run yourself a warm bath.
- The most helpful way is to train your mind through mindful self-compassion practices to change the way you behave. And to allow yourself to become a wise and compassionate woman. Keeping a diary is great to keep track of your responses and feelings as you do your compassion practices.
- The secret is, to be honest with yourself without judging. That way you're beginning to be wise. And you are taking responsibility for developing greater compassion towards yourself. Remember it's OK for it not to be perfect. This diary is your place and doesn't need to be shared with anyone.

**DAY**

**TYPE OF PRACTICE**

**TIME AND LENGTH**

**OBSERVATIONS**

**Monday**

*Walk in the park*
*10 am; 30 minutes*
*I noticed I needed some time alone. It felt good to be in nature*

**Tuesday**

*Visualized my Compassionate Self*
*8.00 pm; 15 minutes*
*This was hard, and my image came and went*

## Wednesday

*No time today too busy*
*Only thought about this at the end of the day*

## Thursday

*Loving Kindness Meditation*
*8 pm; 20 minutes*
*It was good to slow down and focus. I felt calmer*

## Loving Kindness Meditation

If there is only one compassion practice can you fit into your busy life, then this it! One of the first meditations is the Loving-Kindness meditation or in Buddhism the Metta Bhavana. When I first started my meditation journey in 1995, I was taught this meditation alongside mindful breathing meditations. It remains a practice that I do several times a week, and I can feel the difference it makes to me on many levels - physical, emotional and metal.

Loving-Kindness meditation focuses on developing feelings of goodwill, kindness, and warmth. Today research backs up this ancient meditation practice and how it can have profound effects on your health and sense of wellbeing. This meditation enhances our other compassion practices.

Barbara Frederickson[6] and co-workers found that practicing a loving-kindness meditation daily over an extended period can increase positive feelings. Excellent news for us as these are often in short supply when the menopause symptoms threaten to take over. These include feelings of increased joy, gratitude and hope. These positive emotions, in turn, help us to feel a higher purpose in life and decreased illness symptoms. Loving-kindness meditation can help to improve emotional regulation and this, in turn, helps us gain some control over our mood swings, and it can reduce physical pain.

Studies have shown practicing Loving-Kindness meditations can help us manage our stress better and can even slow down aging.

Something that so many of us feel anxious about during the menopause. We know that stress decreases telomere length, tiny bits of your genetic materials, that are a biological marker of aging. Women that practice Loving Kindness Meditation had longer telomere length compared to age-matched controls! An additional incentive to get on your meditation cushion!

Personally, the most significant benefit I see from this meditation practice is that it can help to curb self-criticism. In my mindfulness business and when interviewing women for this book, I found self-criticisms to be a typical behavior that is often rooted in women's psyche. Our sense of self-changes as our body's change, many women become critical and loathe these changes that they have low locus control over. Our outwardly projected society exacerbates this self-criticism where looks determine so much of whether we feel accepted and good about ourselves. A study by Shahar et al.[7] found that Loving Kindness Meditation was useful for in reducing self-criticism and associated depressive symptoms. These changes were lasting even up to 3 months post-intervention.

There are many versions of the meditation but here is the one that I resonate with the most:

*Become comfortable in your chair or cushion, sitting with a relaxed but straight, posture, with your shoulders relaxed.*

*Allow your hands to rest in your lap and close your eyes*

*Bring awareness to the body.*

*Open to whatever is experienced in the body, at this moment*

*Connecting to the breath, observing the breath as comes in out of the body, the belly gently rising and subsiding with each breath*

*In this practice, we'll be cultivating loving-kindness and knowing that we all have this natural capacity for lovingkindness.*

*That loving kindness is a natural opening of a compassionate heart, to ourselves and others.*

*We begin with developing loving-kindness toward ourselves allowing our hearts to open with tenderness,*

*Now, let yourself to remember and open to your goodness.*

*If you have cultivated an image of compassionate self, it may help to use this now if that allows tender feelings of kindness to flow more easily*

*And, as you experience this love, notice how you feel in your body. Maybe you feel some warmth and let a smile come to your lips.*

*Resting with this feeling of open, unconditional love for a few moments*

*Allow yourself to relax in loving kindness. Breathe it in and breathe it out, invite in feelings of peace and acceptance*

*Now wish yourself loving kindness.*

*You're invited to alter these phrases or to choose whatever words express your wishes of loving kindness*

*May I be filled with loving kindness*

*May I be held in loving kindness*

*May I feel calm*

*May I accept myself as I am*

*May I be happy*

*May I know the joy of being alive*

*Now you can broaden the circle of loving kindness by recalling someone who is close to you.*

*Someone whom you care for*

*In your heart feel your appreciation for this dear person, and begin to direct loving-kindness towards them*

*May you be filled with loving kindness*

*May you be held in lovingkindness*

*May you feel calm*

*May you accept yourself as you are*

*May you be happy*

*May you know the joy of being alive*

*Now bring to mind a "neutral" person. This is someone you might see regularly but don't know well. It might be a bus driver, someone who works at a local shop*

*Bring this person to mind now, and repeat the words of loving kindness*

*May you be filled with loving kindness*

*May you be held in lovingkindness*

*May you feel calm*

*May you accept yourself as you are*

*May you be happy*

*May you know the joy of being alive*

*Moreover, now, if it's possible for you, recall someone with whom you've had a complicated relationship.*

*Seeing if it possible to let go of feelings of resentment and dislike for is for this person.*

*Reminding yourself to see this person deserving of love and kindness.*

*As someone who feels pain and anxiety as someone who also suffers.*

*Seeing if it's possible to extend to this person the words of loving kindness in your mind*

*May you be filled with loving kindness*

*May you be held in loving kindness*

*May you feel calm*

*May you accept yourself as you are*

*May you be happy*

*May you know the joy of being alive*

*Finally, allow your awareness to include yourself, the dear one, the neutral person. And then the tricky person and last all living beings, humans and animals living everywhere*

*May all beings are filled with loving kindness*

*May all beings are happy*

*May all beings find joy*

*And now, bringing this practice to a close by coming back to extending compassion to yourself. Sitting for a few moments reflecting on the loving kindness that has been created here.*

## In Summary

- Self-compassion is treating ourselves like we would a best friend who was suffering. When it comes to compassion, the only downside is that you're not doing it yet. If one of your goals is to manage the effects of the menopause, then start with being more compassionate towards yourself. When you give first to yourself, you'll get back even more.
- A short daily practice is a place to start. Every day you can start the day by setting an intention to do at least one kind thing for yourself. Start small but do it. Ten minutes a day of relaxing, taking a short walk or another activity that is all about giving back to yourself. As you embed this practice into your life, you will notice how it lift your sense of self-love.
- Gratitude during menopause is not always a natural strategy when we're feeling the effects of the menopause. But gratitude helps you to manage the menopause experience better both on a physical and emotional level. I would like to encourage you to write at least ten things you are grateful for every day. Yes, I know that sounds a lot. But once you start you will be amazed at how much

goodness there is in your life even when there are tough days.

- Loving-kindness meditations (the Metta Bhavana) is a transformative meditation practice that can change your life for the better. Practicing it daily for several weeks can make a deep and lasting change to your sense of self-compassion and alter how you relate to others. You have nothing to lose by making this your daily meditation practice and everything to gain.

- Compassion provides us with the courage to meet the menopause and work through many painful and uncomfortable symptoms of the menopause. It helps you in becoming the next version of you. Older, wiser and more beautiful. Rather than seeing compassion as something fluffy you will see that through kindness towards ourselves we can find peace amid change. The journey to self-compassion can move us in profound ways.

# CHAPTER 7

# WE ARE WALKING EACH OTHER HOME

*I have come to drag you out of yourself*
*And take you in my heart*
*I have come to bring out the beauty*
*You never knew you had*
*And lift you like a prayer to the sky*
*If no one can recognize you, I do*
*Because you are my life and soul*
*Don't run away, accept your wounds and*
*Let bravery be your shield*
*It takes a thousand stages*
*For the perfect being to evolve*
*Every step of the way I will walk with you*
*And never leave you stranded*

*Rumi[1]*

## Chapter 7.1 Loneliness and the Menopause

For some women, menopause may be a time of isolation. It can be that friends and family members do not always understand what you're going through. Or give you the support you need. A recent survey conducted by the British Menopause Society[2] (BMS) highlighted that more than a quarter of women (26%) said that they felt less outgoing in social situations and felt more isolated (23%). Over a third (34%) reported that they were less social since experiencing menopause. And a further third (32%) said they no longer felt like good company.

These findings reflect the conversations I had when researching this book. Many of the women spoke about losing interest in their social life and how all they wanted to do was hide. Some of this was because of not feeling attractive or feeling ashamed about issues like weight gain. And that hot flashes caused anxiety. Also, they often were too exhausted due to lack of sleep to go for a night out. Anxiety attacks and fluctuating moods also play a role in why so many women feel like not being social. They feel they have to force themselves to socialize. Or they start inventing excuses to give to people, so they do not have to go out. These two stories shared with me are typical of the way many women I spoke with felt the menopause had changed their way of interacting with the world.

*"I used to love hanging out and shopping. Because of the anxiety and how the symptoms make me feel there are times when I haven't been out socially for months. My girlfriends keep trying to get me to hang out, but I don't want to anymore, or at least right now I don't. I only come home now and stay in unless I have to go out. I try to get out when I'm having a good day. Other than that, I'm usually in."*

*"I want to be home where I feel safe. I too am scared of fainting or having a severe anxiety attack and people looking at me like I'm crazy. I used to love going out before the menopause kicked in. Now I go where I have to go and get home as soon as I can. It sounds crazy when I say it, but it's how I feel. I wish I didn't feel this way."*

If you've always been an extrovert, you may be surprised when you suddenly feel like spending more time alone. The menopause is a reflective period in many of our lives, and that may affect your social life. In many cultures, there is a time-honored tradition of withdrawing. Don't jump to the assumption that you're depressed. But, a woman's risk of depression can go double or even quadruple during the menopausal transition and therefore it is essential to be aware of this and seek professional help if your withdrawal starts to create significant problems.

One of the biggest complaints that women have during perimenopause is the sense of having no one to talk to about their symptoms. There is still taboo associated with this stage of life. People don't want to think or talk about getting older. We're also living in a society where it can be uncomfortable or even embarrassing to bring up sexual health. And sadly that some women can even feel that their doctors are dismissive of their symptoms. As one woman recounted "I was told that I was 'too young' for menopause all because I hadn't hit a particular age." Many doctors have limited formal menopause training and means that women often have to look to support themselves if they can't easily find a menopause specialist.

Hormonal changes may result in part the cause of the depressed moods and feelings of wanting to withdraw from social situations. Identifying what a menopausal symptom is and what are 'true' mood changes, depression or anxiety can be confusing.

Depression and depressed mood around the time of expected menopause is more likely to occur because of a range of factors including:

- prior episodes of depression
- significant stress in your life
- a negative attitude to things happening in your life
- dissatisfaction with your relationships
- low self-esteem
- poor body image
- poor lifestyle such as little exercise or a high intake of alcohol.

Emotional health around the menopause is also highly to be influenced by previous experiences with prior traumatic events. Women often seek counseling at menopause and might want to work through traumas they have before experienced, as this time of life difficult past events can resurface.

Research suggests women who have surgical menopause, and early menopause is more likely to experience clinical depression than women who have menopause at the expected age, influenced by the sudden drop in hormones that comes with surgical menopause. It might also be related to the illness that caused the surgery in the first place, such as a cancer diagnosis.

Knowing that depression is more likely to occur during perimenopause, and early postmenopause can help you identify worrisome symptoms and act sooner. Hormone therapy can be the right choice for some women, but according to recent research, it is by no means a blanket approach. Non-drug strategies can be used to support depressive symptoms. These include lifestyle interventions, such as managing stress and boosting physical activity.

## Chapter 7.2 Opening Up To Friends and Family

Living in isolation, particularly during stressful life experiences, has never been recommended for your health and happiness. Going through menopause in isolation is no exception. It's important to talk to your doctor when changes occur with your body. But we need to be encouraged to speak with our friends or family as well even when the physical changes are personal or could be perceived as embarrassing. One of the most challenging issues for loved ones is being left out and feeling like they have to tread carefully, not sure of what reaction to expect. Those who are less sensitive get annoyed and impatient. Because the symptoms of menopause are so misunderstood, you may have a challenging time even explaining what you are going through, let alone how it is making you feel on an emotional level.

For example, vaginal dryness, decreased libido, urinary incontinence, mood swings, anxiety, fuzzy thinking, and depression are all symptoms that many women report during the menopause. Many women do not tell the complete story even to people close to them.

Seeking support during menopause from family and friends is as crucial as consulting your physician.

Let's start with friends first. Women form strong bonds with other women, and on the whole, we are good at sharing the intimate aspects of our lives. Sharing your menopausal feelings, fears, and concerns with your friends are amongst the most positive things you can do for yourself. Chances are, they are experiencing it, too. The experience may not be identical. But you will receive the most important thing, and that is validation that there is nothing wrong with you and that what you are experiencing is a normal part of the menopause transition.And that is music to the soul.

Another important aspect of talking about your menopause experience with your female friends is uncovering solutions to relieve symptoms. Your doctor may offer a few, but your girlfriends may have ten or twenty answers. Having more answers gives us the ability for us to take control of the situation. There's nothing more powerful than knowing other women that have gone through menopause and survived!

## The Unplugged Mummy Brain

During menopause, a woman's brain goes through massive changes. Dr. Louann Brizendine[3], the author of The Female Brain, wrote, "The mommy's brain unplugs." Menopause means a decline in the hormones that have boosted connection and driven nurturing behaviors and the inclination to avoid conflict at all costs. There are extra factors that may contribute to a lack of communication. These include common medications prescribed to help menopause symptoms, such as antidepressants, mood stabilizers, antihypertensives, and drugs for blood pressure.

The menopause is a precarious time for a family. Our society is built on the family unit, and that unit is formed on a mother's estrogen. Her role as a cleaner, peacekeeper, cook, diary-keeper, school liaison officer and at least some of the time as a doormat, is the cornerstones on which the family is constructed. The depletion of estrogen throws at the very least a curve ball into the family.

Facebooks is full of outpourings from teenagers whose mothers have changed (overnight) into someone they describe as a psycho or a monster. Although she has spent years caring for their every whim, all they have noticed is that she is no longer doing it. And that is not only inconvenient but painful. But, it is as if nature calls time on the intense mothering phase and it is calling time on your kids too. "Grow up," I shouted many times when my son asked me to make a dental appointment or do the ironing or drive him somewhere. "Grow up, do it yourself."

Menopause is a time when you can allow your children to take more responsibility and let them grow up. Not being so involved in your children's lives, frees up time to focus on yourself. It can deepen the quality of your life, which in turn heightens the quality of your interaction with your children.

Behaving this way applies if you have no children of your own. Our instinct is to mother, whether that is your partner. Or you are the woman who 'mothers' her friends or colleagues, watching over them. 'Mothering' can be in any relationship where we do not allow the space for another to take responsibility for themselves. When you stop mothering others in the menopause, do you create more time and energy for yourself? YES!

Explaining and sharing what you are going through can allow you to forge adult-to-adult relationships with your children. You are still their mother, but through this sharing, they can also gain an awareness that you are an individual with needs.

**Sharing Your Menopause Experience with Your Partner**

Sustaining long-term relationships is challenging in today's culture. The divorce rate is close to 50% in many countries, and for those over 55, it is rising. Fewer couples are willing to remain in challenging relationships if it means living for years with frustration and unhappiness. Given this scenario, it's essential to address the issues that cause friction. The menopause can be one of those issues. And we cannot underestimate the impact that menopause and its symptoms have on women, their relationships, particularly their close intimate relationship.

Midlife stresses at work, empty nest syndrome or caring for elderly parents can also contribute to a declining libido. Throw in the physical signs of aging and its impact on attractiveness and the last thing on a menopausal woman's mind is communicating, let alone sex. When a woman feels unsupported in a relationship while managing this change,e leaving the relationship may appear like her only solution.

Many women are reluctant to share what they're going through with their partner. They can feel embarrassed over their mood swings if their symptoms affect sexual intimacy. If you don't share what's going on with your partner, they may take it personally, and connection deteriorates affecting not only intimacy but also affection and day-to-day communication. The BMS survey also found that 51% of women said that the menopause had changed their sex lives. And around 40% saying that they didn't feel as sexy since experiencing the menopause

About 10 % of women see an increase in their libido, and this was my personal experience. It sounds incredible, but at times it was frightening and uncontrollable. My sex drive which was always high "skyrocketed." It would come in cycles where I would have no interest in sex and then the mid-cycle I was insatiable! This surge in desire lasts for about three days every cycle; It was crazy!"

Testosterone is the hormone that is linked to libido for women and levels slowly drop over time. Testosterone interacts with other hormones and the increased libido in some perimenopausal women could be due to "the relative balance and interaction of these hormones. It may also be due to women feeling less anxious as sex becomes less linked to the possibility of pregnancy. This explanation of increased libido coming with drop-in fertility and a lessened fear of pregnancy makes perfect sense. After all, the largest sexual organ in the body is the brain.

In writing this book, I also had the opportunity to talk to some men about their feelings around their experiences with their partners' menopause journey. Every one of them wanted to know what they can do or could have done to be more supportive. Many of them feel powerless to help their partner.

They want to know how they can help to ease the discomfort that comes from hot flashes, mood swings, and sleep disturbances and the rest. When it comes to sexual intimacy, they want to know how they can make it a better experience for their partner. They often do not understand that sex has diminished not because their partner no longer finds them attractive but because it is may be painful to have sex. The men I spoke with wished they have been better informed.

Intimate relationships can be very complicated. And a multitude of factors affects their longevity and health. But, honest and open communication will improve the relationship. Men are natural problem solvers, and they want to help, so provide them with direction and let them support you.

Deep listening is a way of opening up to communication with your partner (and family). When we can communicate like this, it is a big relief. To listen to you and the other person must be 100% present. We all have this ability, but we seldom use it because we are usually lost in our past or future thoughts and ideas. Mindfulness helps to be present and non-judgemental. We must learn as the Buddhist monk Thich Nhat Hanh[4] says to be space. Space can hold everything, that's when love can enter. When we let go of preconceived ideas to be present in the heart of the other person.

Can you and your loved ones learn to listen to each other? Even if you repeat yourself, try to understand what each person is saying and also what is being left unsaid, and you may be able to see the critical point. And be able to ask the right questions to help each other. The aim of deep listening is understanding. When someone is suffering if he or she can find one person with the willingness and capacity to sit quietly beside them and listen, that is a great encouragement. Whether what they have to say is easy to hear or shocking it is not rejected. When we train ourselves to listen to understand and when we listen deeply we manifest great love and great compassion which in turn relieves our suffering.

## Chapter 7.3 Breaking the Isolation Through Mindful Connection

Learning to connect with those nearest and dearest to us boosts our sense of well-being. And when done with compassion it can help to break our sense of isolation which comes over us during the menopause. Strong social connection leads to better physical and emotional health at a cellular level.

But, when life feels difficult, it can be hard to extend love and to care towards others. But connecting with others even through small moments can transform your life. The American psychologist Barbara Fredrickson[5] is well known for her work on positivity and love that she calls the "supreme emotion." Love in this context isn't a romantic relationship or the love you feel for your family or even between best friends. Instead, she defines it as the moment-to-moment experience of warmth and caring that we can feel with any person in everyday interactions. Something she refers to as "shared positivity."

Research has shown that when we feel a connection with another person, our brains tend to "go in sync" with each other physically. Anyone who has been in a meaningful conversation with another person knows the feeling of intimacy it can create. Quite literally your brains are firing in the same patterns, in the same parts of the brain. This mirroring is what creates a "positivity resonance" a shared emotion that can make you feel alive and upbeat.

The hormone oxytocin also plays a crucial role in connection, and it has been found that oxytocin helps us to read social cues better. It helps us to be more generous, caring and open. All of which foster trust, a critical ingredient in connection. Oxytocin is referred to as the "tend and befriend" hormone for its role in promoting caring feelings and behaviors during positive social encounters. Thereby reducing stress, lowering heart-rates and producing a warm fuzzy feeling. Two people feeling positivity resonance will have synchronized releases of oxytocin, which makes them feel even better about each other and themselves.

The vagus nerve that runs from the brain to many parts of the body, including the heart and lungs. It is designed to increase the love and feelings of connection. This nerve is the sensory network that tells the brain what's going on in our all our vital organs. It is made of thousands of fibers, operating far below the level of our conscious mind. It plays a crucial role in sustaining wellness. It is an essential part of the parasympathetic nervous system, which is responsible for calming us after a stress-related "fight-or-flight" adrenaline response. There are a few simple things we can do in our daily life to improve our vagal tone

*Take care of your gut. The enteric nervous system or the gut's nervous system connects to the brain through the vagus nerve. There is increasing evidence of the effect of the gut microbiota on the brain. Eating right helps to keep your gut flora stable and healthy and this, in turn, improves vagal tone.*

*Alter heart rate variability. Studies have shown that alternate nostril breathing can improve our heart rate variability. It sounds odd, but it's simple, and it works. Yogis have been doing this for centuries.*

*Place your ring and pinkie fingers at your left nostril and your thumb at your right nostril.*

*Block the left nostril using your ring and pinkie fingers and inhale through your right nostril.*

*Block the right nostril with your thumb and exhale through your left nostril.*

*Inhale through your left nostril, keeping the right nostril blocked.*

*Continue for nine more rounds.*

*Reduce jaw tension. The jaw is related to the vagus nerve, and tension or misalignment of the jaw can cause low vagal tone. By stimulating the tissue where the vagus nerve branches out behind the ears, you can decrease the compression the tissue often has at the base of the skull. My most loved exercise that also fits well with making you feel connected is to Smile. Try to have the widest smile you can without feeling tightness or pain. Then open your jaw an* extra *bit. Inhale through your mouth, then exhale while releasing the smile. Repeat up to 10 times. This stretch helps to eliminate stress and tension held in the facial muscles, upper and lower jaw, and neck.*

From a connection perspective, vagal tone is involved in everything from talking to eye contact with facial expressions and even your ability to tune in to other people's. It also plays a role in coordinating heart rate and breathing. The more coordinated these are, the better your "vagal tone," which turns out to have all kinds of health benefits.

All of these internal systems work beyond our conscious control. But, we can tap into them and reap their benefits. These are my top ways of cultivating better vagal tone. They can support well-being during perimenopause and menopause when we want to shut out the world.

## Sing, hug, and dance

Of course, by cultivating more positivity resonance in our lives, we can improve our vagal tone. One of the most effective ways revolve around using the loving-kindness meditation as described in Chapter 6. This meditation practice in which you send out positive wishes to yourself and people in your community. Along with gratitude practices or conscious focusing of your attention toward positive interactions with others will if practiced regularly make a difference in your health, outlook, and relationships.

One way that I like to practice 'positive resonance' is to look for moments of love and connection in my day. Here's what happened when I did dedicate a day to seeking out those moments of positive resonance. Moreover, you will see that hugging is my favorited way along with giving people some of your time, looking them in the eye and listening to them. OK, it can feel uncomfortable at first to hug people, but once you are in the flow, it feels fantastic. You can try this experiencing micro-moments of love in your day.

*Started the day with breakfast with a good friend at a local coffee place and had a big hug before breakfast and another one at the end*

*I rocked up at my co-working place and caught up with two co-workers whom I had not seen since before the long summer break. We all hugged each other.*

*It was still morning, and already I had three hugs under my belt. Research on hugging indicates we should aim for eight a day to feel at our best. I now had a mission to achieve those hugs.*

*Even so, it was only just gone midday, and the score stood at: -*

*Micro-moments of love 3, Hugs 4*

*In the afternoon I headed off to the gym. A lady whom I recognized from my other gym classes smiled at me, and we had a chat about her holiday. Then I got into a class with my favorite instructor so there lots of high fives and moments of connection even if he was pushing me on.*

*By the afternoon I was at: -*

*Micro-moments of love 5*

*Hugs 4*

*Before heading out to the choir, I had two phone calls one with my son and one with my partner adding another two micro-moments of love and connection*

*I went to my choir, and as it was the first time back after the break. It was a fantastic opportunity to connect with our choir leader and two friends. And it meant three micro-moments of love and three hugs.*

*The fantastic thing about music, singing, and dancing, is that you meet some happy people. A few of the guys high fived me, and we shared two moments of laughter and joy.*

*So, what did I learn from this day?*

*It doesn't take much to have 'positive resonance 'moments in your day. Without changing my day but by becoming more aware of micro-moments of love I transformed my day completely. I worked out I had a total of twelve micro-moments and seven hugs, not quite the magical eight but still impressive, and I felt connected, calm and joyful.*

For me, a day like this demonstrates the power of mindful connection. It's not making a significant event that will change your life. It's about experiencing everyday events and enjoying those experiences. Whether they are with family, colleagues, friends or strangers. Every encounter is an opportunity and the way we approach those opportunities makes all the difference between how we feel within ourselves and in breaking our sense of isolation.

## Chapter 7.4 Build Your Tribe to Survive

People who are more connected to others have high self-esteem. They are more empathic to others, more trusting and cooperative. In return, others trust and connect with them. Social connectedness, thus, generates a positive feedback loop of social, emotional, and physical well-being. Unfortunately, the opposite is exact for those who lack social connectedness. They not only experience declines in physical but also psychological health which in turn leads to further isolation.

As women, we have a natural tendency to want to stick together and protect one another. Women are generous in their ability to give support to each other. We want to feel as if we are making an impact. Helping to make a difference in the lives of other people. Many women enjoy living their lives through a cause that serves the advancement and acceleration of societal needs.

In a menopause context, we are seeing more and more women coming together to support each other through the menopause. Both emotionally and practically. There are some great menopause resources in the form of blogs, podcasts, and websites that provide an understanding of precisely what's going on with your body. As well as current medical advice and finding camaraderie with other women.

It can also be helpful to join a group either face to face or on Facebook. If you find yourself facing the menopause alone, you may want to think about finding a menopause support group. They can help you stay positive throughout menopause. You can meet friends that will last for the rest of your life.

The first place to start looking for a menopause support group could be at your doctor's office. Many doctors will know of groups such as these. If you live near a women's clinic or you may want to call them. It may take a little searching to find a group near you.

If you have searched high and low and still cannot find a group, you can always consider starting your own either on Facebook or in your local area. You will be surprised at the overwhelming support and response you will get. It may take a little time and effort, but it will be worth it in the end

The group often expect you to share your menopause story. They will only be wanting to get to know you, which may be uncomfortable at the start, but open up to the women in the group, and you will get tremendous support from the group experience. You will likely find that many women are going through the same experiences as you, keep an open mind and have a good time!

## In Summary

- Social isolation is not uncommon amongst perimenopausal and menopausal women. Often we feel like withdrawing from the world because of our physical or psycho-social conditions. But, isolating ourselves from others can lead to a further decline in our mental and physical wellbeing. And we can find ourselves trapped in a vicious cycle.
- It is critical to be able to share how we feel emotionally and physically during this time in our lives. If sharing your feelings and experience with menopause difficult start by talking with someone you know who will listen without judgment. This person may be a family member or a best friend.

- With long-term relationships so fragile in today's culture, it's essential to talk about your menopausal symptoms with your partner. Why suffer alone? Menopause does not have to be a solo act, but a shared experience. You might be surprised how understanding and supportive the people who care for you can be. Start talking. It's a good beginning.

- Practicing deep listening with all your attention and open-heartedness without prejudice allows you to hear what the other person is saying and also what is being left unsaid. You can reduce a great deal of emotional pain and suffering of your own and other people through deep listening. Cultivating a gentle deep listening practice with your partner and family members brings about a transformation in your relationships.

- Moreover, we need definitely to break the stigma of sex in the menopause and beyond. We've grown up in a culture that views sex as something for the young and beautiful. We need to see opportunities to see older couples being romantic in a healthy way, not a humorous way.

- Stimulating vagal tone through breath and smiling is an added way to reduce our stress and as part of opening up to positive micro-moments. Every day without changing anything we can connect with people all around us. And use those moments to reduce our sense of isolation and loneliness. Moreover, of course, the more hugs we can get in the better.

- On a broader scale connecting is a form of increasing our knowledge. And it gives you a sense of what you're in not only one experiencing these are symptoms as it is important for your well-being. And your ability to go through the menopause able to place your experiences in context, as well as being able to reach out, get guidance and emotional support. There are great online resources, forums and more that are uplifting and positive. Try to avoid those that the websites where they only want to talk about problems as this reinforces our negativity bias.

# CHAPTER 8

# A BLUEPRINT FOR DAILY MINDFUL LIVING

*You need to be content with small steps*
*That's all life is*
*Small steps that take you every day*
*So, when you look down the road it all adds up*
*And you know you covered some distance*

*Katie Kacvinsky[1]*

## Chapter 8.1 Bringing Awareness to Your Day Every Day

It is easy to become trapped in your usual patterns of behavior. And this can lead to distorted thinking around your menopause experience. That, in turn, can lead to reactive feelings like anxiety, fear and overwhelm. Mindfulness teaches you to peel back all these layers of distorted thinking. To develop a closer understanding of your day to day behavior. And the pattern of your menopausal symptoms can teach you how to make small behavioral adjustments that create micro-moments of calm in your day.

### Your Menopausal Patterns

Becoming more attentive to our menopause symptoms and experiences helps you to manage your menopause more effectively. An effective way is to keep "a daily diary" that enables you to understand your symptoms. Use this to uncover which activities, aggravate or ease your symptoms and which have no impact at all. To live mindfully, feeling calm and at ease, means creating a personalized plan to help you manage your symptoms. And to know the activities that make them better or worse, as well when and where you need to adjust. It could mean taking more regular breaks to prevent exhaustion. Doing grounding or breathing exercises before or during a stressful meeting at work to help you manage a hot flash.

Approach this diary with a kind-hearted awareness. And remember not to criticize or punish yourself. See this as a way to establish a baseline from which you can make an adjustment where possible. Moreover, if you do find that you need to consult a healthcare provider the documentation of your experiences will help you to communicate your unique situation more effectively with your clinician

## Example of a Diary:

Scale the intensity 0 = none, 1= minimal, 2 = moderate 3 = moderately intense 4 = intense

Symptom

How Long it Lasted

Activity You Were Doing

Time of Day

Rate the Intensity

## Managing Your Energy

Menopause often leaves us feeling sapped of energy. This drop-in energy can make daily tasks seem daunting. It can leave you feeling exhausted and lacking in perspective. These feelings can contribute to low mood. The primary cause of fatigue is changing hormone levels. Estrogen, progesterone, thyroid, and adrenal hormones are all important for regulating cellular energy, which when compromised leads to fatigue. Add into the mix symptoms like night sweats it's not surprising many women find themselves suffering from chronic insomnia, which is a major contributory factor in fatigue. Fatigue exacerbates menopausal symptoms including anxiety, lack of focus, and a lack of confidence. You can find yourself in a vicious circle.

Mindfulness won't remove the factors that lower your energy, but it can help you to manage them better.

## Mapping Where Your Energy Goes

One of the most effective ways is to deepen the awareness of the different dimensions of your life. Giving you an insight into the things in your life that lift or drain your energy.

The different dimensions of your life include the following categories:

1. The Physical Environment which includes your home, your possessions, your workplace, your car or places in nature
2. Relationships include people close to you and in your broader network
3. Money include your actual income, savings, spending habits, debts and budgets
4. Technology which includes physical products like your phone as well as social media and other virtual places
5. Your Body includes your appearance, how you talk about your body, diet, exercise
6. Your Soul includes the routines and places you go to wind down, your emotions

*Grab some paper and find some quiet time and ask yourself some questions.*

*Where do you spend your energy across these categories? Go into detail in each of the categories in detail and explore further:*

1. *What things in this part of my life uplift me, bring me joy, make me feel great?*
2. *What kind of things to do I do that drain my energy? Are some of these here out of habit even if I know they don't serve me?*
3. *What could I do to get rid of some aspects altogether?*
4. *Are there things I can't change and need to find a way to accept?*
5. *What support mechanisms to I have and how can use them better?*
6. *What gives me energy*

7. *What is missing that could make this area of my life better?*
8. *What are the first steps I'm going to take to make a change?*

A typical chart might look a bit like this for a few of the categories:

| CATEGORY | UPLIFT ME | DRAIN ME | DROP/ACCEPT | SUPPORT | MISSING | FIRST STEP |
|---|---|---|---|---|---|---|
| Physical Environment | Going for a walk in the park near my office at lunchtime | Clutter everywhere | Donate or sell all the clothes you haven't worn in the last year. | Tidy up my desk area. Finish painting the back bedroom | A special place in your house where you wind down | Invest in a piece of kitchen equipment that encourages healthy eating |
| Relationships | Chatting with my sister on Sunday afternoons | Friends that constantly complain | Stop taking phone calls from people who don't uplift you | Identify the friends who are positive and find ways to spend more time with them<br><br>Sign up for classes or groups with uplifting activities like a choir or a meditation group | | Say no to someone you usually say yes to or if you tend to say no trying saying yes, a little more often |
| Technology | Music apps that suggest new things that are fun to dance to | Spending 8 hours a day online | Turn off my mobile during and remove social media notifications | Download an app to help track how much time you spend online and where | Replace social media apps with ones that encourage you, e.g., to walk, meditate or cook | Learn a new way to be more effective with your emails or go on a digital detox for a week |

Put out something that symbolizes your new goals - an object, a daily intention chart. Put your table somewhere visible and track your progress. If you have a difficult period, start to feel down in the dumps or uninspired. Look and remind yourself of what lifts you

## Dropping the Resistance

The menopause doesn't always give us what we want. If we try to fight against it, if we resist the changes and the difficulties, the more they persist and the harder we make it for ourselves.

140

I know from my journey of resisting and pushing back and struggling when my world felt like it was unraveling when everything seemed to be going wrong that my resisting only made the problems ten times worse. My health deteriorated with rising blood pressure, and my weight ballooned. Mentally my fears, anxieties, emotions, and fantasies controlled every waking moment. And although I could fall asleep without any problems, I woke up several times a night. Then there was a tendency to want to check my phone. Thoughts would intrude that kept me awake for hours, and by the morning I was exhausted. My confidence felt eroded, and my sense of self-worth was on the floor. My approach to coping with the menopause, and the work pressure I was under, was to resist and block out the changes. I did this by making changes to my physical appearances like regular Botox and fillers to hold back the wrinkles. Along with several glasses of wine, every night to 'help' me to wind down. So, I crashed to sleep on the couch at 8 pm but still woke up in the night.

The reality is many women are exhibiting some form of blocking behavior (e.g., pushing against the discomfort), it can appear in many ways. It can take the form of exercising too much, excessive shopping or drinking, over the use of social media or even talking too much.

Sometimes we do the opposite, we drown. We start playing the victim, losing interest in everything, withdrawing from others, blaming everything and everyone. All in an attempt to try to find a way to cope with the menopause.

But, as I became more skilled at mindfulness, as I quit resisting, and things started to fall into place. I learned to stay with my primary experiences and feel the changing nature of the menopause without needing to create a chain reaction of thoughts.

When things seem to be crashing all around you, the way forward is to seek balance. If you feel like you want to block out physical discomfort, then listen carefully to your body sensations. See if you soften any tension using the breath. If you feel like your thoughts are overwhelming you then broaden your awareness. Seek out pleasant little things you see the bloom of a fresh flower or feel a cool breeze on your neck. Notice that as you focus on these sensations how everything is changing all the time.

Instead of trying to control the outcome let go of your preconceived notion of how things are supposed to be. See the changing nature of life and ease into the flow. Get out of your head and learn to listen to your heart and soul. I had to learn the hard way, and even though I have stress in my life, everyone does, but I can choose how I respond to it. And I talk to myself in a kind voice, and I'm more accepting of my body. I've learned to appreciate the simple things in life like the sunshine on my back, a hug. Or a cup of tea with a girlfriend, a walk in the forest, a good book, time with my son. I learned to feel gratitude. To focus and let in the goodness which is all around us. And to practice acceptance and learn from the challenges that will always come with being human.

## Chapter 8.2 A Focus on The Fundamentals

It is essential to care of yourself in the critical areas of eating, sleep and exercise as you go through the menopause. Mindfulness helps us to become more aware of ourselves. And my personal experience was that as my practice became a habit deepened, I started to 'want' to eat more healthily. I slept better and found exercises that I enjoyed. But, as we all need a helping hand here some extra things you can do to support yourself further to move mindfully through the menopause

### Eating:

Many of us have a complex relationship with food, and as we go through the menopause, it's an opportunity to evaluate that relationship. I've personally never been someone who diets, but many of my friends and the women I've interviewed have dieted for years with varying degrees of success. During the menopause, you can pile on the weight and feel tempted to keep dieting as you did in your 20s and 30s, but now is a beautiful time for you to stop.

Moreover, if you've never been on a diet, this isn't the time to start. Diets often don't work, and restricting food can cause you to feel unnecessarily hungry. Dieting may slow your metabolism, leading to more weight gain or at the least not shifting it.

Instead, this is a time to reappraise you're eating habits and follow a few simple guidelines[2]

- **Control Your Blood Sugar**: High and lows in blood sugars can trigger hot flashes as well as leading to weight gain. The foods that can cause your blood sugar to rise are of course sugar. Plus, refined grains like the ones found in pasta, white rice, white flour. Choose whole grains like brown rice or wholemeal pasta that is slower to digest due to the fiber. These will lead to a more gradual increase in blood sugar. Balance your meals. Each meal should include a protein, fat, and carbohydrate. Eating this way will slow down digestion and work to keep blood sugar levels even. Refined starch and added sugars are the biggest drivers of weight gain at any age. So, reducing or best eliminating these from your diet will help maintain weight post-menopause. If you've mapped your menopause symptom, then you can get a sense when your symptoms occur, e.g., hot flashes at 11 am. Moreover, it is possible to use food to help minimize these occurrences. For example, a snack of an apple with nut butter can help.
- **Your Microbiome**: The bacteria that populate the digestive tract is the microbiome. And is very important for hormone balance. There are bacteria that either enhance or prevent the elimination of excess estrogen that often can occur during the menopause. The bacterial balance can also influence our metabolism and any subsequent weight gain. Eating fermented foods (like kefir, sauerkraut, and kimchi) and having a varied diet can support a healthy microbiome.

If eating in a balanced way is proving to be a challenge, then consider going on a mindful eating course. This type, of course, teaches you specific techniques that support your healthy eating journey.

## Exercise

Exercise helps you to feel healthy and active, to appreciate what your body can do and how good you feel when you move it. In addition, exercise provide many other health benefits, including reducing the risk of heart disease and type 2 diabetes. Moreover, exercise can also help with menopause symptoms. It can help to reduce weight gain and aids with sleep if it is not done too late in the day. In a study of over 500 women, who exercised during the menopause transition vs. a control group, the non-exercisers gained an average of 4 kg. Strength training and weight-bearing exercise also help maintain bone density, which helps to prevent osteoporosis.

From a mindfulness perspective exercise is an excellent way of connecting your mind and body. This connection helps to take us out of our ruminating and reduces our stress levels. When you are exercising, you might notice that there is often no time for thinking about the past or the future. You can be 100% in the present moment.

Besides yoga and running, which I love to do, I teach mindful movements, and they have become one of my favorite tools. The Vietnamese Buddhist monk and teacher Thich Nhat Hanh[3] has developed exercises based on Yoga and Tai Chi movements, which are worth investigating. Other moves I particularly like are from a company called Smart Break[4]. They provide automated workout videos, exclusively designed for office workers who sit too much. The key is to build movement variety into the typical workday through smart activity breaks. The 3-minute breaks make you feel better instantly. You can run Smart Break on your smartphone, tablet or workstation - anytime, anywhere!

The movements can include getting up from your chair every hour and reaching your hands to the sky. Never mind if you feel silly doing them, do them or better still co-opt some of your family and colleagues to join in. These simple and effective practices help to reduce stress and tension. When done as part of broader mindfulness practice, these movements can address mental, emotional, and physical stress. What I like best is about mindful movements is that they are wonderfully simple. When I do them, I can't help smiling. Please give them a go, and I hope they bring you joy.

My final piece of advice around exercise is always doing what you can, do it often and enjoy these moments.

## Sleep

If there was only one key area you could commit to the I would always choose SLEEP. Rest is critical and without a good night's sleep it the next day is s struggle. Most of the women I've spoken to have reported having interrupted sleep. Frequently waking up drenched in sweat. Many also reported feeling anxious during the night. Like they had a huge weight pressing down on their chest. Sleep disturbance is frequent during the menopause transition and is in part related to an imbalance between hormones. The delicate balance between Progesterone and Estrogen. Also, low blood sugar levels during the night can be a trigger of early awakening and disrupted sleep.

Mindfulness supports in several ways to improve the quality of our sleep. The practice of mindfulness brings our nervous system into balance, calming the sympathetic while strengthening the parasympathetic, helping us to feel calmer and more relax both mentally and physically. When we feel calmer, it helps us to drop off to sleep and minimize the chance of becoming wide awake in the middle of the night. Mindfulness also helps us to bring more awareness to our habits. It helps us and to establish a good bedtime routine that supports deep restorative sleep. These are my top tips that are backed by some good science to help you to achieve a better night's sleep, especially if you find you are having trouble sleeping due to insomnia or night sweats.

- **Stick to a Routine**: Don't chop and change. It's essential to have a good routine of going to bed and getting up at the same time even on weekends. It helps to settle your sleep patterns. There is no magic number when it comes to duration, but most women should aim for 7-9 hours a night. Try keeping a diary or try tracking your hours with an app.
- **Manage the Light**: Melatonin is our sleep hormone. Back in our caveman days, when the sun went down, our melatonin levels would rise, telling our bodies it was time for sleep. We would wake with the sun, which would decrease our melatonin levels. Melatonin matters when it comes to, and we need to manage our light.
- Unfortunately, in our modern world, we are disassociated with natural cycles of light because of indoor lighting and our reliance on gadgets. Most screens project blue light, and smaller screens especially so. Moreover, that's why it's essential to dim the lights an hour before bedtime. Transition to dim lighting an hour before bed. Light dimmers, lamps or candles, and notice the impact this makes as you wind down before bed.
- **Keep It Cool**: This one's essential given how we menopausal women seem to overheat very quickly. Scientists believe that a more relaxed room is more conducive as it works with the body's natural temperature drop at night. Aim for around 18 degrees in the bedroom. Keep the place cool and cover yourself with a warm duvet. Pop on socks if your feet get cold at night. Wearing socks reduces night waking. Just make sure they don't have a tight band?
- **Wind Down**: I am a fan of baths before bed! Not only are they relaxing, helping you to wind down and get into a relaxed state before dozing off. One of the reasons we have problems with our sleep is that when we're stressed our bodies are tense, and that makes harder for our minds to relax.

- Practicing relaxation before or in bed helps with restlessness and facilitates sleep. Some people find listening to the gentle sounds of nature helps them get to sleep. Journaling at bedtime helps if your mind is still racing, as you can get all those thoughts out of your mind and down onto paper.

- Gentle body-based meditations help the body to let go of tension and tightness aid restful sleep. I'm a huge supporter of using Yoga Nidra meditation to bring on a relaxing night. I started using a Yoga Nidra meditation a few years ago and to support me to fall back to sleep if I woke up during the night. Yoga Nidra is such a powerful technique. It very quickly stopped the waking up thing! I felt so refreshed in the morning. Now I make sure it's part of my night routine.

- **Cut the Caffeine, Alcohol, and Snacks:** Caffeine tends to lead to poor sleep. And not unsurprisingly people that have insomnia, often consume a lot of caffeine. Why not try a relaxing herbal tea near bedtime? A small study found that 10 minutes of active exercise was more energizing than caffeine. So next time you're craving that mid-afternoon coffee, go for a quick power-walk instead.

- Although alcohol can make you feel sleepy, the effect is short-lived. Moreover, can make you wake-up after a few hours unable to get back to sleep. Alcohol also prevents the body from entering the deeper stages of sleep where the body does most of its healing. Growth hormone is the body's primary repair hormone, and alcohol inhibits 75% of this hormones release. Also, drinking also interferes with melatonin release.

- Snacking, or eating high-fat foods, is associated with shorter and poorer sleep. So tonight, try to make sure you have a nutritious sit-down dinner, at least two hours before bedtime. Foods like rice, oily fish like tuna or salmon, kale and chickpeas are all healthy foods that can help to improve sleep.

- Eating late at night, especially a heavy meal, can adversely affect your sleep. If you feel the urge to snack, there are some food that helps because they contain certain amino acids or minerals that trigger our bodies to make sleep-inducing melatonin. Believe it or not, Grandma was right when she wanted you to have a milky drink before bed-time. If that's not your thing, a handful of almonds or walnuts or a banana can also do the trick. Also, they can prevent your blood sugar levels from dropping too low that cause you to wake up and find it hard to get back to sleep.

## Chapter 8.3 Creating Anchor in a Storm

When you go through the menopause, you will have "one of those" days or moments many times over. As I know from my experience how the mind takes over and you can become preoccupied with unhappy and unhelpful thoughts and feelings. It helps to have an anchor for the mind, a place to go which is neutral. You can return yourself to the here and now, calming the mind and soothe the body.

Already in the book we've discussed developing an Inner Resource, the value of the three-minute breathing space and grounding your feet onto the floor or you bottom onto a seat and feeling held by gravity. These are types of anchors. But, there are also other ways to anchor the mind that has been very effective. My personal preference is the breath because it's always with us. It's easy to notice; it operates without much effort as an antidote to stress as well as supporting our general physical and emotional wellbeing.

### Breathing

When you use breathing consciously it allows helps to regulate your blood pressure, heart rate, digestion, and many other body functions[5]. When you wake at night, feeling like there is a weight on our chest, or a hot flash threatens to derail you, the breath can be used to manage these stressful situations. Breathing deeply is a way of stimulating the parasympathetic nervous system. Amazingly our bodies know to do this naturally when we take a deep breath or sigh.

Many of us in the Western world breath shallowly and are sometimes described as "chest breathers". Breathing this way is often rapid and shallow and results in less oxygen going to the blood and in turn fewer nutrients to the tissues.

Abdominal breathing sometimes as called diaphragmatic breathing is good for your physical health because it improves the flow of blood and lymph. Abdominal breathing also is an excellent way to stimulate the relaxation response resulting in less stress and an improved sense of well-being. If you practice the abdominal breathing exercise then over time you will notice that your energy levels improve, a real plus during the menopause when so many of us feel extra tired.

*Abdominal Breathing Technique*

*Place one hand on your chest and the other on your belly. Take a deep breath in and notice how the hand on the abdomen rises higher than the one on the chest.*

*Exhale through your mouth, then take a slow deep breath in through your nose hold it for a count of 7 (or as long as you are able)*

*Slowly exhale through your mouth for a count of 8. Gently contracting your abdominal muscles to completely remove any remaining air from the lungs. It is important to remember that deepening our breath comes not from inhaling more air but through fully exhaling it. A general rule of thumb is exhalation should be twice if inhalation.*

*Repeat the cycle, so you've taken five deep breaths. Once you are familiar with this breathing technique, then you can add to it simple words like breath in, breathe out or peace and calm.*

Abdominal breathing is one of many breathing exercises. If you are interested in exploring these further, I recommend looking at the work of Ed Harrold[6], coach and former director of yoga at Kripalu in the US. His 30 day-plan outlined in his book "Life with Breath" or UK-based Rebecca Dennis[7] author of "And Breathe." Breathing is, without a doubt, the essential anchor to learn before exploring other techniques. The more you practice, the more natural it will become improving the body's internal rhythm and helping you to calm any situation.

## NLP Anchoring

My years of working with clients have made me realize that there are times when focusing on the breath can be difficult. If you have experienced a traumatic event focusing on breathing can bring up bad memories. Also, if you have an intense dislike for the way your body looks and feels you may feel a shortness of breath when your attention is too close to your body. In these instances, I recommend choosing a difference anchor. In neuro-linguistic programming or NLP, anchors are used to producing a state of mind, e.g., calm or confident.

Anchors can be visual, auditory or kinesthetic. You can use a combination of anchors such as seeing a symbol in your mind's eye. An example of this is hearing something said like the words calm and relaxed. While at the same time you place your hand in a specific place like on your heart or rubbing an earlobe. Or hold an object like a stone. You may have seen people pinging elastic bands on their wrists. They are anchoring using the band.

Setting up a basic NLP Anchor[8] is easy to learn. Here are a few steps to get you started.

*Basic NLP Anchoring*

*Select a feeling that you would like to have in a situation, e.g., You might want to feel confident when a hot flash takes hold in a meeting at work*

*Take a few moments to remember a time when you had that confident feeling. Be sure to choose a strong example.*

*Close your eyes and remember that feeling in detail. Can you recall how that confidence looked, the colors in the situation, the sounds or a word that enhances the feeling?*

*When your feeling is at its most intense, you create a physical association by making a gesture, e.g., squeeze your thumb and forefinger together Or you make a fist, rub your earlobe or a small object or ping a band on your wrist. Then as the feeling subsides, release your 'anchor' and relax. Repeat examples of having that feeling, e.g., confidence and use the same gesture. Doing this will teach you to mind to 'fire off' the anchor when you want to feel confident.*

Imagine how supportive it would feel if you could, in a moment, go from feeling anxious to feeling decisive and confident in the middle of a hot flash during work.

## Chapter 8.4 Living Mindfully

Learning to find your optimal stress levels and ensuring you have the resources and habits that give you enough capacity in the metaphoric tank and bit in reserve for when things get stressful means you can go through the menopause feeling less stressed and overwhelmed. But just as you can burnout you can be more than OK. Mindfulness can help you to flourish and thrive through this time of your life

These four steps sum up the critical steps to living with mindfully day to day supporting you living well.

**Be Present** - this is the foundation of mindfulness and living with greater ease and a sense of calm. It means coming back to the present moment again and again when our minds want to race into the future or re-hash the past. It means realizing that everything is transitory. Even our menopause symptoms are changing moment by moment. It is developing an open awareness to appreciate what life provides. Presence is cultivated by bringing mindfulness into our daily routines. By making mindfulness a habit. Often women say to me, 'but I don't have the time" but we do have the time to check social media 150 times a day or watch hours of Netflix. Mindfulness can start with the commitment to a single short practice that is adapted to the time you have available. Everyone has a few minutes and attaching this practice to something you already do can assist to make it become a sustainable habit.

*Choose one routine activity in your daily life and make a deliberate effort to bring the moment to moment awareness of that activity. Possible activities include brushing your teeth, showering, taking out the rubbish or washing up. Focus on the activity 100%, no multi-tasking. Pay attention to what this feels like. If you choose to brush your teeth what does the toothbrush feel like on your teeth and gums? How does the water feel in your mouth, what does your toothpaste taste of, bring you to mind back if it repeatedly wanders, as it inevitably will?*

**Pace** - we live in a world where having it all and doing it all and often all at once means we're running on empty. And if you live this way for a prolonged period, then it can have significant detrimental effects on your health. Pacing teaches us to accept that you cannot achieve everything in life all at once and that you need to make time for rest and drop the multi-tasking. By creating and using your menopause diary to help you cut activities that exhaust you or exacerbated any menopausal symptoms. Pacing means permitting each phase of the menopause from early peri-menopausal right through to being post menopause. If you can learn to pace, you find that you gain awareness and a sense of perspective.

**Prioritize** - this means being conscious of your values and going back to the energy uplifters that you identified earlier. Focusing on these, when faced with the endless priorities that confront you every day, helps to prevent feelings of exhaustion and overwhelm at home and work. In practical terms, this means letting go of things that drain you. Learning to delegate to others, or not doing things that are meaningless. It gives you permission need to ask "What matters? And then to direct more energy towards these valued activities.

**Be Open to Change** - As you become more mindful, you are developing a greater awareness around your menopausal symptoms and discovering the activities that support you to live in a balanced way. You will find it easier to have the courage to make any changes to your situation with compassion. This focused attention may mean that you reach out for more help at home. You might change career direction or begin new morning and evening routines that support you.

## In Summary

- Learning to live mindfully in our daily life means mindfulness comes off the meditation cushion and fully into to your life where it can support you at moments when you need it the most. Cultivating a greater understanding of your menopausal symptoms and when they occur helps you to find balance. It helps you to have mechanisms in place to avoid allowing your physical and mental conditions to have more hold than they should.
- Learning that we what resist persists. And that reacting to the unpleasant aspects of the menopause can create more problems than it solves.
- Knowing your energy drainers help us to avoid exhaustion and burnout. Building up your energy givers, those you already have and new ways to bring positive energy into your life, give you support you to live well.
- Eating healthily, getting enough sleep and exercise are essential elements to wellbeing. If these habits are not already in place, then the menopause can be an excellent time to establish them. These habits that support you going forward.
- Finding an anchor during the problematic menopause moments can support you especially if you feel you are losing control. Breathing prevents stress becoming mapped onto your body. Gentle, simple anchors like word, memories or objects can create a sense of calm and ease in stressful situations.

As you become more mindful through practice daily, realize that you can go through the menopause with less stress and pain. If you can learn to live mindfully, you will have more choice over your mental and emotional state. You will gain a greater sense of inner freedom. The ability to go with the flow, calmly knowing and accepting the changes. Of course, that doesn't mean that every moment or even every day is fantastic. But it does mean that you can be less reactive, less cynical, more resilient, kinder and wiser. Remember to be kind to yourself, let in the good and spend some time each day paying full attention to whatever you are doing. In this way, the mindful menopause can be a blueprint for your life going forward.

# CHAPTER 9

# THRIVING THROUGH THE MENOPAUSE AND BEYOND

*Thoroughly unprepared we take the steps into the afternoon of life; worse still, we take this step with the false assumption that our truths and ideas will serve us in hitherto. But we cannot live the afternoon of life according to the programme of life's morning; for what was great in the morning will be little at evening, and what in the morning was true will at evening have become a lie.; Carl Jung[1]*

## Chapter 9.1 You Have A Choice

The most beautiful thing about menopause is you get to choose how you respond to the changes as you go through them. You may not feel the need to change your mindset, and that's ok too! But, it is a choice time. We can stay as we are if we like or we can "go" and create our new space. How you go through the menopause by managing your choices is your most significant challenge and opportunity.

But, you will find that on the other side of mastering the physical and mental difficulties there is a life of balance and harmony, a wonderful life. Everything in this book has been about mindful choice and mindful practice. Making a conscious choice in any situation where the menopause symptoms want to dominate will in some measurable way to increase your sense of well-being and contentment. Mindfulness can improve your sense of optimism, resilience, and control over your own menopause experience.

Reflecting on how mindfulness helped me the most significant step was that I started to notice changes from having daily meditation and mindfulness practices. I felt "peace" once I decided to stop feeding the constant churning over of thoughts The indulging in the addictive emotions and putting a halt to all the drama that surrounded every moment in my life. I gained the insight that I had a choice of whether I engaged in these habits.

I'm not saying this is a natural thing; real mindfulness is difficult. I know this firsthand. But, mindfulness works. Moreover, as you may have gathered through the book, I don't consider mindfulness only to be "paying attention to the present moment." I believe it to be living in the present moment. To unraveling and changing those habits that keep your mind from being quiet, still and clear.

So how do you "decide" what is more peaceful? Well, if you've come this far, you understand that you will gain much from making different choices. You need to learn how to calm the mind down. This why a formal meditation (and patience) is key. I have proposed several different meditations throughout the book that teach you to detach from the constant stream of dialog that runs through your mind. Practices that allow you to touch the stillness beneath the chimp chatter. That stillness can show you an alternative to chaos. You will only feel this stillness for a few brief moments in meditation. But you'll know it when you touch it, though it may take some time to get there.

Daily mindfulness exercises will help you to tap into that same level of peace. Yes, it's possible to feel the same peace of mind that you feel in meditation in the supermarket, at a meeting or when you wake up drenched in sweat. Stillness is always there, beneath the surface of the chimp chatter and the uncomfortable body sensations. And no, you're not checking out, you're present and engaged. You're just not attached to the drama that accompanies the menopause. But, mindfulness isn't about being perpetually happy. It's about the complete acceptance, the willingness to feel what is here to be explored, without trying to resist or control it. It is 'being with' life's challenges in a mindful way, remaining calm in the midst of it all. Avoiding excessive grasping at positive emotions and rejecting the negative.

To manage your internal narrative, the one that is critical, judgmental and blaming you can use the COAL process developed by Daniel Siegel[2]. COAL stands for Curiosity, Openness, Acceptance, and Love. In this practice you can say to yourself:

(C) " Hmm, look at how I responded; now I'm mindful of my response."

(O) "okay that's not the first time I behaved this way; it happens too often

(A) " it happened again, but this time I'm mindful of my behavior."

(L) " while I don't approve of my behavior, I know that I care about people and in my heart, I'm a good person."

By exploring your narratives in this way, you begin to recognize new opportunities and make different choices in your life.

Being in a mindful state needs an unrelenting curiosity about anything that might surface. Curiosity helps you in becoming more present, aware and living life intentionally. Achieving mental control takes practice and, in my experience, it happens bit by bit. Once you understand how mental choices work, you can start by not engaging with the thoughts and emotions that cause pain. Like such as anger and fear, and instead, choose to respond to any given situation with compassion and bring an understanding of your negative states of mind, as we did in Chapter 5, and what that does to your state of mind. You may find that as you stop one mental habit, you can apply a similar approach to another. Making changes becomes increasingly more accessible.

When you face something that brings up a reaction, you can stop and decide if I go down this road, will I end up angry, sad, filled with self-loathing? Could I take a different path, one that is non-reactive, and choose to stay in a more peaceful state? I have a choice.

Most people don't believe they have choices and pre-mindfulness I would have agreed with them. Choices weren't even an option; I was victim to my thoughts and emotions. But, since becoming more mindful, the journey has been and still is fantastic! I make a choice every day to respond rather than react, to rest in stillness and clarity of thought. And you can too.

I've known and coached many people who gain so much from mindfulness only to stop practicing once they felt better, and unsurprisingly they revert to their old habits to see their problems resurface. Mindfulness only works to the extent that you practice it! There some critical steps that help you to keep going when practicing feel difficult. That is why linking the ongoing practice not only to habits, situations or problems you'd like to change or remove but to your values is critical. To work on uncovering and creating a life aligned with your inherent strengths. To your authentic self.

## Chapter 9.2 Knowing Your Values and Strengths

Perimenopause and menopause signify a new chapter in a woman's life. At this stage, you may find a renewed sense of purpose. The decline of progesterone and estrogen makes you less inclined to be caring for others and more focused on your needs and what's important to you. You can find yourself wanting to seek out the new and become more involved in the world. Jill Ruddock[3], the author of the book The Second Half of Your Life, says it's a familiar feeling for women to wake up one day and realize that their lives have been about satisfying other people but that this life has been dissatisfying for themselves. It's not that you need to change, you have changed.

Many of the women I interviewed who were post-menopausal made changes on the deepest levels. They resigned from dissatisfying jobs and started a business focused around their passion. Some women who had been unhappy in their marriages and say, 'I'm not going to put up with this anymore.' Women start more than 60 percent of divorces in their menopause years according to a survey conducted by AARP Magazine[4]. Not that I'm advocating this because each person is different and in a different situation.

Mindfulness helps you to gain self-awareness and clarity about yourself, your values, strengths, passions, and qualities so you can claim your purpose. If you don't know your purpose, these steps below can help you uncover it.

## Know Your Strengths.

Strengths can be defined as "a pre-existing capacity for a particular way of behaving, thinking, or feeling that is authentic and energizing to the user, and enables optimal functioning, development, and performance."

Every person has signature strengths, but they may not be aware of the advantages they have. But they play a significant role in our sense of well-being and happiness. Strengths reflect our true individual core and allow us to be our best selves. A tremendous free downloadable tool is the VIA Strengths Survey[5] can help you to increase your awareness of your strengths and create a way for developing and optimizing your strengths.

I encourage you to get a friend to also do the VIA survey for you. As we know, it's easy to be critical of ourselves. But our friends see positive qualities in you that you sometimes ignore or even don't understand.

## Determine Your Values.

Values can help you to the answer to the question: "If you could choose to have your life be about something, what would you choose?" or what is important to you? Values help you to become aware of the direction of your life and to see where your life is aligned with what you have importance. Also, this can be a starting point for developing strategies that promote behaviors in line with your values.

Although values are essential (e.g., exercising, eating healthily), our behavior may not be consistent with these values. We might be spending more hours on social media, working at home in the evening than we want to. The first step to becoming aware of the discrepancy between values and actual valued living, a good starting point for making value-based changes during the menopause.

There many ways that you can increase your awareness of your values and the extent to which you live them. Traditional approaches include The Bull's-Eye Values Survey that assesses values, values-action discrepancies, and barriers to value-based living.

I use the Hierarchy of Values of approach that comes from Brahma Kumaris spiritual centers. It looks in depth across 13 aspects of your life.

## STEP 1.

1. What do you fill your personal and professional space with most? E.g., computer, photos, trophies
2. How do you spend your time first, second and third?
3. How do you spend your energy and what energizes you the most?
4. How do you spend your money?
5. Where are you organized the most?
6. Where are you most reliable, disciplined and focused?
7. What do you inwardly think about most?
8. What do you visualize the most/?
9. What do you dialogue with yourself about most?
10. What do you talk to others about in social settings?
11. What inspires you most?
12. What are your most consistent long-term goals that are coming true?
13. What do you love learning, reading, studying or listening to?

**STEP 2.**

Once you have written three answers for each, i.e., 39 responses in total, you'll see a pattern even though you may be expressing the same values in diverse ways. Then you can start to note the answers that are most repeated and later the second, third and so on creating a ranking of your values.

**STEP 3.**

You can then write about how your life would look if you were living life as you want to be and compare how far off the mark you are in each category. Following that write down what is between you and living your c life as you want to, based on your values. When you think of life, how do you want to live, and the values that you would like to put in play, what is getting in the way of you living that kind of life? And to what extent do these things prevent you on a scale of 1 to 5.

Now that you have given yourself the time and space to explore and know your strength and values, you can begin to find your purpose. Or as I like to call it your Hearts Deepest Desire

## Chapter 9.3 Find Your Hearts Deepest Desire

What fills your soul? There's nothing that will make you live your life with more health, more energy and heart than waking up each day looking forward to living your hearts deepest desire. Studies have shown that if you live life with passion and on purpose, you're less likely to suffer from health issues. It can also give you and have increased longevity. Living this way can reduce the possibility of heart attack and stroke. Cut your risk of Alzheimer's by more than half, improve sleep, decrease inflammation, and repair your DNA to slow aging. A life with a purpose is the key to happiness, vitality, and health.

What is your Heart's Deepest Desire[7]? It is a felt sense, the heart's longing rather than something that is difficult to express in words alone. It is like the code to living a fulfilling, purposeful life that is unique to you. Letting your heart become a beacon that steers you towards what feels right and true. Every heartfelt "yes" or "no" is a call from your most authentic self that can show you the way home to wholehearted living.

It is reasonable to feel unsure of "what exactly is my heart's deepest desire"? One way I have found helpful to get a sense of this, is to ask yourself the question "what is life is asking of me?" and then becoming still and tune-in to the whisperings that emerge. I have found that journaling and meditation on my values and strength have been the most effective ways to allow me to listen to the deeper intentions within me. To reflect on how I wish to express myself in the world.

What I find moving in creating a Heart's Deepest Desire is that we are NOT being asked: "what do I want from life or what do I want to achieve in life." But rather, there's much more a sense of "life is living through me." For me, when I live aligned with my heart's deeper desires, I have more of a sense of ease and inner harmony within me even when challenges or difficulties arise.

As you explore this question, don't worry if nothing comes to you straight away, it can take time for the essence to emerge, but the overtime more specific intentions of how to live your life purposefully will develop

## Creating Your Hearts Deepest Desire

Imagine you are 90 and looking back upon your life. What are the moments that you are most grateful for? What were your greatest successes personally, professionally and spiritually?... Are there any unfulfilled desires that if you could turn back time, you would add to your life?

Now imagine yourself going back in time and inserting the fulfillment of these desires. Use all your senses and emotions to help anchor this into a new memory

Now, as you once again look back upon your life, is there a common thread or theme to your hearts desires that might be revealed as your life's purpose?

Take your time with this. Allow it to come from the heart. It might at first come more like a feeling rather than thinking.

When you phrase it keep it in the present tense, positive and concise.

When you meditate, you can recall the Hearts Deepest Desire at the end of your practice. You imagine what your daily life is like with the Hearts Deepest Desire as if it is already true. To allow images and what I call "future memories" to emerge. These show how your Hearts Deepest Desire positively impacts your relationships, your daily activities, your health, and wellbeing.

As we open to the experience of our purpose becoming real, we are creating new neural connections in our brain. As Rick Hanson[6], author of Hardwiring Happiness wrote, "Emotions are like rocket fuel for building new neural circuitry."

When we want what we want, it becomes as beautifully put in the Brihadaranyaka Upanishad;

"You are what your deep, driving desire is.
As your desire is, so is your will.
As your will is, so is your deed.
As your deed is, so is your destiny."

The forces of destiny are ever present, beating in our very own hearts.

Will you heed the call?

It's important to remember that our Hearts Deepest Desire will naturally evolve and that it is valuable to list intentions and action steps and include time-bound deadlines to ensure success. In this way, we are actualizing the Hears Deepest Desire (HDD) through meaningful action steps in our daily lives.

To help this along, I love making a vision board to bring my HDD to life. What is a vision board? It is a visual representation of your HDD, of whom you want to be, the steps you want to take and the things you want to have in your life. Moreover, it's a daily reminder of those things. And that's very powerful because where your attention goes, your energy flows.

## Chapter 9.4 Step into The New You

As we come through the menopause and out the other side, we're older and wiser. We have a lot to contribute! For many of the emotional, physical and social changes post menopause has been energizing.

Now that the hot flushes and the brain fog have stopped I feel like a new person. I've got more energy, more and more drive. I've got the confidence to go in new directions in my work, and I've gained back my interest in the way I look and dress which might sound trivial but is essential to me. I feel ready to take on the next half of my life.

Many women experience a rush of energy after the menopause which anthropologist Margaret Mead[8] called "menopausal zest." This rush of energy, both physical and psychological, that many women feel after menopause makes it a natural time for women to take a fresh look at their closest relationships, their jobs, their health, and the ways they want to spend their energy. Having mindfulness in our lives lets us do this from

Margaret Mead described what it feels like "There is no more creative force in the world than a menopausal woman with zest and this has been backed up by psychological research that found most women felt more energized at 60 than at 40 with noticeably improved cognitive function and memory. Moreover, depression in women has been found to decrease after the menopause.

Stable hormones and life changes often come together. Our children grow up, and we gain more time and energy as they leave home and post the menopause the balance between estrogen and testosterone shifts. Moreover, that gives us more drive, more drive, more zest."

This time marks the end of the menstrual cycle, which for many of us is a cause for celebration. PMS affects 85% of women in some way, with symptoms that can become worse during perimenopause due to hormonal fluctuations is over. Your moods improve as you find a sense of balance in the body, which in turn, leads to better sex post-menopause. And not just because the hot flushes and sleepless nights have gone but being free of the menstrual cycle also helps.

Many women would openly admit that we weren't that interested in sex during the menopause and in fact, I felt decidedly unsexy most of the time. I thought that was it, that I'd would never have sex again. And that was sad that something that had been very important to me was over. But, these days sex is better than it's ever been. Of course there are lifestyle factors alongside biological changes. A woman's sex drive can be higher because of her testosterone levels. But also because this is a stage where many people start new relationships. Or if in a long-term relationship the empty nest there is a freedom to have sex and have more time for each other.

Post-menopausal zest has a positive impact on many parts of our lives. It gives us a new impetus to exercise, and to try out new stuff, like yoga, running. This impetus, in turn, makes us feel better and boosts our energy levels.

A great meditation to support bringing our new life into reality is one I call Dream Manifestation. This meditation puts you in the mindset of living your Hearts Deepest Desire, to look for things that will help you along this path. It can help make your purpose and your dreams a reality.

*Begin by relaxing your body, body part by body part. Start with the top of your head, then move to your forehead. Relax the front of the head, the back, and the middle, too, if you can. Then bring your attention to your eyes, relax the left and then the right eye. Then your nose, your jaw, mouth, and lips. Step by step focus and relax all of the muscles of the face,*

*Bring your attention to both arms at the same time and legs too. Finally, relax your feet, from the ankles all the way down to your toes.*

*Scan through your entire body noticing, breathing into, relaxing any areas of tension.*

*Bring your attention to the sensation of the breath as you breathe in and out. What do you feel? What do you notice? Breath in and out of your nostrils normally but be alert to the sensations you feel as the breath comes in and out of the body.*

*Then silently repeat to yourself, "My heart is open. I open my heart. I am good, I do good, and I am loved."*

*When we do this type of heart-opening meditation, we feel calmer. And the tone of our vagus nerve increases as we activate the parasympathetic nervous system. In other words, we stimulate our rest-and-digest response.*

*Now we're ready to start manifesting. Choose one or two goals, whatever you wish that is aligned to your Heart's Deepest Desire to pursue the career you've always dreamed about, to fall in love, to travel, whatever you'd like!*

*In meditation, imagine what your life would look like if this goal were already accomplished. What do you see? What colors? What shapes? Where are you? What are you wearing, what do you smell, who is with you? Stay with this. It can be hard at first. Over time, the details will start to fill out. Repeat with another goal*

*When you are ready slowly begin to return to the room, feel yourself sitting on the chair, attune to the sounds around you and when you're ready gently open your eyes.*

Of course, this doesn't mean we have eliminated stress or stressful situations from our lives. But this new energy combined with mindfulness practices can help us to enjoy our life more skillfully. You can stop sweating the small stuff and embrace the next half of your life to live. Stop holding back you can take more chances. Many women including myself switch careers, turning passions into income. Reignite their relationships or start new ones go on their travel or take up new pursuits that they been putting off on hold. There's is no time like the present to build a life that's is aligned to your Hearts Deepest Desire. Using your strengths and living according to your values. It is an exciting time to be a woman!

# APPENDIX.

## Using This Book as an Eight-Week Course

| Week | Theme and Chapter to Read | Meditation Practice | Other Practices |
|---|---|---|---|
| 1 | Chapter Two: Listening to the Body | Body Scan: Do this every day for a week | Create an Inner Resource |
| 2 | Chapter Three: Getting Calm and Clear | Breathing Anchor: Experiment with this in different contexts several times a day. Try it for a week | Slow Down: Take one activity a day and do it slowly |
| 3 | Chapter Four: The Wisdom of Our Emotions | Opposite Emotions: Meditate once a day for a week | Mindful Movements |
| 4 | Chapter Five: Rewiring the Negative Thinking | Leaves on Stream: Meditate at least once a day or whenever you feel thoughts are taking control | Let Be, Let Go, Let In |
| 5 | Chapter Six: Becoming Your Own Best Friend | Loving Kindness Meditation: Do this at least once a day for a whole week | Visualize Your Compassionate Self |
| 6 | Chapter Seven: We Are Walking Each Other Home | Loving Kindness Meditation: Meditate at least once a day for six out of seven days to stimulate vagal tone | Daily Hugging Ritual |
| 7 | Chapter Eight: A Blueprint for Living | Three Minute Breathing Space: Do this several times a day | Map Your Energy Flows |
| 8 | Chapter Nine: Thriving Through the Menopause and Beyond | Dream Manifestation Meditation: Daily for six out of seven days | Hearts Deepest Desire |

# NOTES

**Chapter 1.**

1. Faulds, D. Go In and In: Poems from the Heart of Yoga ( Peaceable Kingdom Books 2002)
2. Loehr, A. (February 2016). "How Menopause Silently Affects 27 Million Women at Work Every Day". Fast Company
3. Snelling, S (2015). "When Menopause And Caregiving Collide." Next Avenue
4. Bodhipaksha (2014) "What Is Mindfulness"? Wildmind Buddhist Meditation
5. Tolle, E. The Power of Now (Namaste Publishing, 1997)
6. Fontane Pennock, S (2015) "22 Mindfulness Exercises, Techniques & Activities". Positive Psychology Program

**Chapter 2.**

1. Gilbert P (2010) Training Our Minds in, with and for Compassion. The Breathe Project
2. Panay N, Briggs P, Kovacs, G . Managing the Menopause: 21st Century Solutions. (Cambridge University Press 2015)
3. Germer, C.K, The Mindful Path to Self-Compassion. (The Guildford Press 2009)
4. Miller, R. Yoga Nidra: A Meditative Practice for Deep Healing and Relaxation (Sounds True 2010)

Brown, L (2017) "Surviving menopause with some (self) kindness. Practicing self-compassion can help manage menopausal symptoms". University of Melbourne

**Chapter 3.**

1. Segal Zindel V, Williams M. J, Teasdale J.D (2002) "Mindfulness-based cognitive therapy for depression: A new approach to preventing relapse" Guilford Press.

2. Harvard Medical School Memory and Menopause
3. Smith C, Smith R, Wesley D, (2017) "Yoga for the Brain." CreateSpace
4. Harrold E, (2017) " Life with Breath: IQ + EQ = New You." Go Be Great Inc
5. Ophir E, Nass C, Wagner A.D "Cognitive control in media multitaskers" PNAS September 15, 2009, 106 (37) 15583-15587

## Chapter 4.

1. White K "Open World: the collected poems 1960-2000" (Edinburgh: Polygon, 2003)
2. Nuffield Health (2014) "1 in 4 with menopause symptoms worry about coping"
3. Thich Nhat Hahn "Peace in Every Step" (Rider 1991)
4. Angelou M "The Complete Collected Poems of Maya Angelou" (Penguin Random House LLC 1986)
5. Pullen, W Running with Mindfulness: Dynamic Running Therapy (DRT) to Improve Low-mood, Anxiety, Stress, and Depression (Penguin Random House 2017)
6. Q. Li, "Forest medicine," in Forest Medicine, Q. Li, Ed., pp. 1-316, Nova Science Publishers, New York, NY, USA, 2012.

## Chapter 5

1. Gary Hennessey
2. Hardwiring Happiness: Rick Hanson Rider & Co 2015
3. Cognitive Defusion: An Empirically Supported Strategy To http://www.washingtoncenterforcognitivetherapy.com/wp-content/uploads/2017/01/

## Chapter 6.

1. The Essential Rumi Translated by Coleman Barks (Harper, San Francisco, CA, 1961)
2. Neff K "Self-Compassion: The Proven Power of Being Kind to Yourself: (2011)

3. Homan K J, Fuschia (2017) S M " Self-compassion and physical health: Exploring the roles of perceived stress and health-promoting behaviors" Health Psychology Open

4. Training Our Minds in, with and for Compassion Paul Gilbert 2010

5. Emmon R "Thanks! How the New Science of Gratitude Can Make You Happier. ( Houghton Mifflin 2007)

6. Fredrickson B L, Cohn M A, Coffey K A , Pek J, Finkel SM . "Open hearts build lives: positive emotions, induced through loving-kindness meditation, build consequential personal resources." J Pers Soc Psychol. 2008 Nov;95(5):1045-1062

7. Szsepsenwol S, Zilcha-Mano H, Levi-Yeshuvi Z, Levit-Binnun H. A wait-list randomized controlled trial of loving-kindness meditation programme for self-criticism. Clin Psychol Psychotherapy. 2015 Jul-Aug;22(4)

## Chapter 7.

1. The Essential Rumi Translated by Coleman Barks (Harper, San Francisco, CA, 1961)

2. British Menopause Society Survey Fact Sheet (2017)

3. Brizendine L: "The Female Brain" (Penguin Random House 2006)

4. Thich Nhat Hanh Mindfulness Bell (2008)

5. Fredrickson, B L. Love 2.0: How our supreme emotion affects everything we feel, think, do, and become: (Avery 2010)

## Chapter 8.

1. Kavinsky K.(2010) "Awaken"

6. Thrive During The Menopause Transition - Annals Behavioral Medicine 2003 Dec;26(3):212-20

2. Thich Nhat Hanh "Mindful Movements: Ten Exercises for Well-Being" (Parallax Press 2008)

3. Smart Break 2018

4. Rakal, D Learning Deep Breathing. Psych Central July 2016
5. Harrold E, (2017) " Life with Breath: IQ + EQ = New You." Go Be Great Inc
6. Dennis, R Breathe. The complete guide to conscious breathing - the key to health, wellbeing, and happiness. 2016
7. NLP Anchoring - Personal Development Training & Resources, Trans4mind.com 2016

**Chapter 9.**

1. Jung C. "The Collected Works of C.G. Jung. The Practice of Psychotherapy (Princeton University Press 2014)
2. Siegel D J "The Mindful Brain: Reflection and Attunement in the Cultivation of Well-Being" (W. W. Norton & Company 2007)
3. Shaw Ruddock J "The Second Half of Your Life" (Vermilion 2015)
4. AARP survey (2004) Divorce and the Menopause
5. VIA Strengths Survey. VIA Character Organisation
6. Hanson R "Hardwiring Happiness: The Practical Science of Reshaping Your Brain and Your Life" (Random House 2013)
7. Douglas A (2015) The Heartfelt Desire Anahata Yoga Therapy
8. Nancy Lutkehaus "Margaret Mead: The Making of an American Icon." (Princeton University Press, 2008)

# RESOURCES

Now that you've gained a taste of mindfulness you might be interested in deepening your practice. I have put together a small resource list of books and websites that can be used as an opportunity to experiment on your own. Retreats and audio-visual material can also be valuable ways to go deeper into mindfulness.

## BOOKS

Burch V, Irvin C (2016) Mindfulness for Women. Piaktus

Dolgen E, Dolgen J (2015) Menopause Mondays. The girlfriend's guide to surviving and thriving. Amazon

Gilbert P, Choden (2014) Mindful compassion: How the science of compassion can help you understand your emotions, live in the present and connect deeply with others. New Harbinger Publications

Goldstein J, Kornfield J (1987) Seeking the heart of wisdom: The path of insight meditation. Shambhala

Kabat-Zinn J (20110 Mindfulness for Beginners: Reclaiming the present moment and your life. Sounds True

Northrup C M.D (2012) The Wisdom of the Menopause. Hay House

Salzberg S (1995) Lovingkindness: The revolutionary art of happiness. Shambhala

Salzberg S (2010) Real happiness: The power of meditation. A 28- day program. Workman Publishing Company

## WEBSITES

www.franticworld.com mindfulness information and practices

www.unmassmed.edu/cfm Center for Mindfulness at the University of Massachusetts. MBSR teaching and research www.selfcompassion.org Self-compassion research

www.mindandlife.org Science of meditation and compassion

www.greatergood.berkley.edu Resources and articles on mindfulness and compassion

www.dharma.org/ims/mr_links.html meditation centers and communities in your area

## RETREATS

A short residential retreat is a beautiful way to deepen your mindfulness practice in a supportive environment. There are many beautiful retreat centers around the world. I enjoy the Triratna Buddhist centers that can be found in many countries and that hold regular retreats in natural environments. You can find more information here https://thebuddhistcentre.com

It is also worthwhile checking out local meditation groups, mindfulness and yoga teachers as many of them run annual retreats as well as day retreats, which are a great mini-break when you want to quiet downtime but can't get away.

# INDEX

# Acknowledgments

I am indebted to my coach Rupy Kaur for her enthusiasm, encouragement, and belief in me. And for her matchmaking skills in connecting with Vanessa Ogden Moss, who with her team, has supported and encouraged me to bring this book into the light.

Thank you to all the women and men who agreed to be interviewed and be case studies for this book. I am grateful that you so generously shared your menopause struggles. Your unique journeys and perspectives of what the menopause is and can be are the backbone of this book. I have changed your names to protect your privacy. But I hope you will enjoy recognizing yourself in the text.

I am especially grateful to my son Thomas for his unerring support and faith in me. To my partner Sigurgeir Kristjansson for agreeing to support the proofreading part. Words cannot adequately express my gratitude.

My practice of mindfulness and understanding of mindfulness would be nowhere if for the ground-breaking work of my teacher Vidyamala Burch at Breathworks. Thanks also to Karen Hall and all my Breathworks colleagues as well as my iRest teachers Stephanie Lopez and Fuyuko Toyata for theeir unselfish support in my mindfulness journey. They have inspired me to find the courage to look deeply inside myself.

I'd also like to offer my gratitude to all my clients who I can't personally thank or name in this book but who have kept this book grounded in the reality of our daily lives.

I would like to thank all the readers who will take these message and practices to their hearts and lives. It is a journey where we together are walking each other home.

Printed in Great Britain
by Amazon

78942079R00107